SUSTAINABLE
LEGACY

Traditional Welsh Buildings and the Environment

SUSTAINABLE
LEGACY

Traditional Welsh Buildings and the Environment

Cliff Blundell

DEDICATION

    With acknowledgment and thanks to all who have helped me with this book, I dedicate it to the memory of the late Nigel Lofthouse, who had to leave the party far too early.

    He never really believed that his love of natural materials and his talent and skill when working with them were an abiding influence on my life and laughed when I told him. I'll bet he's still laughing.

TLC Press
Bryn y Mor House
Cardigan
SA43 1PA

Copyright © Cliff Blundell 2013.

Cliff Blundell has asserted his right under the Copyright Designs and Patents Act 1988 to be identified as the author of this book.

A CIP record for this book is available from the British Library.

First published 2013
ISBN 978-0-9927158-0-9

CONTENTS

Designed by Ian Findlay Design www.ianfindlay.co.uk
Pictures by Cliff Blundell, Louise Noakes & Ian Findlay, unless otherwise stated

Printed by Westdale Press Limited
70 Portmanmoor Road Industrial Estate Cardiff CF24 5HB
www.westdale.co.uk

FOREWORD

BY THOMAS LLOYD OBE FSA

"We are" as Cliff Blundell declares in his Introduction "at a crossroads on the route to better understanding our historic buildings." Such a view will surprise people who assume we have learned by now all there is to know. But this is not a book about learning: it is a book about understanding – understanding how to maintain, love and look after that 'precious inheritance' of traditional Welsh homes which thousands of people own and live in. In short, Cliff is talking about almost every house built before 1919, one third still of the housing stock of Wales, all originally constructed with solid, lime rendered walls, real Welsh slate roofs and wooden windows ... although too often hardly recognisable as such now.

Our ancestors of a hundred years ago would have been equally surprised by Cliff's contention. There would have been no need then for this instructive and sometimes provocative book. Everyone from jobbing builder to grandest landlord would have been familiar with the compendium of long-practiced wisdom that Cliff has reassembled here. If they could have seen ahead a hundred years, they would be laughing or nodding sagely at the trenchant criticisms that Cliff makes of misapplied, off-the-shelf fixtures which grimly adorn the exteriors of so many older houses and the misunderstandings of natural laws of geology and chemistry which upset their underlying structures.

This book is not a manual of fussy affectation for those who enjoy being old fashioned. It is a book of revelation. My much abused old house had, when I first came to it, very old lime render on its front wall and thick cement roughcast on the equally exposed side wall, following alterations in the 1960s. The wind and rain hit both walls vigorously at 45 degrees but only the side wall let in the damp. Now re-coated in lime render, the inside wall surface is dry throughout the worst winters.

And these days you need not just listen to an old convert like myself. John Griffiths AM, Minister for Culture in the Welsh Government wrote an article in the Western Mail on 1st May 2013 stressing the importance of the historic environment to the future prosperity of Wales. He drew attention to the Government's determination to create facilities to help train craftspeople "in the skills necessary for the conservation and maintenance of traditional buildings. This is hugely important for a nation where 34% of the building stock is traditionally built and whose character we do not want to lose." This book is about those last nine words.

Cliff is not some hoary old goat-skinned prophet suddenly appearing out of the wilderness. Other flag wavers for the protection of our everyday built heritage have been trying to get the same message across for years, though drowned out by the commercial powerhouses of the new-build industry. Every Welsh person takes pride in the name of Clough Williams Ellis because of his magical creation of Portmeirion, not appreciating that he devoted as much passionate attention to the preservation of the traditional look of the countryside. Equally forgotten is the message of another Welsh architect, Thomas Alwyn Lloyd (1881-1960), of nonconformist Liverpool Welsh parents, who understood the timeless beauty of the old north Wales landscape and how man had shaped it. His professional life was much devoted to the post-War planning of new towns and villages (the overarching care and sophistication of which have mostly been lost to random alteration) but he had been a co-founder of the Council for the Protection of the Welsh Countryside as far back as 1929 and he wrote a regular stream of articles and pamphlets advising on the best way to build there.

One reads with sad reflection today the wise words of Alwyn Lloyd. In the December 1945 edition of the fine monthly magazine "Wales", he addresses the pressing issue of post-War housing: "What should be our guiding principles in this new building and reconstruction? First we should make full use of our native traditions in design and material. Some critics are in the habit of disparaging these, or even deny the existence of a Cymric architectural heritage." ... "Probably the outstanding feature of Welsh domestic architecture is its simplicity of outline and detail. Buildings take their place naturally in their environment, and good proportions of wall surface, roof and fenestration are invariable. There is little attempt at 'effects' or of standing out from one's neighbours. Hence, the striking contrast of the modern villa of pretentious façade and unsuitable material. When there are pressed bricks, machine-made tiles or large smooth slates, the house never mellows with age, as native structures do, but continues as a harsh scar on the landscape" ... "We are in danger therefore of losing track of a long tradition of workmanship, the revival of which could restore native character to our buildings" ... "The mistake is to think in terms of the single dwelling, however crucial that may be to the individual concerned, and not of the wider community". Almost all this wisdom has fallen on stony ground of course, but the value of its truth still holds good. In Tenby for example a ten year scheme by the Pembrokeshire Coast National Park persuaded all the house owners around the magical harbour to select a paint for their façades from a choice of palettes that would harmonise. The result enhances every house and the entirety of the urban landscape. Look around at other old Welsh towns and contemplate the disastrous introductions of new colours, mauve and lime green on single houses that wreck the whole street.

The language of Clough Williams Ellis and Alwyn Lloyd and others of their time and cultured sensitivity may seem old fashioned now (Herbert North,

Harold Hughes, Iorwerth Peate, Cyril Fox all have proud places in the cause) but their message has not died out. Of our own time, the late Peter Smith engaged the interest of thousands in his magnificent book "Houses of the Welsh Countryside" (1975), while Eurwyn Wiliam's equally inspiring "The Welsh Cottage" (2010) now illustrates the simple beauty of old rural housing further down the social scale. The lack of creature comforts available to their owners may seem ugly to us today, but they never built the garish things that we routinely and with few exceptions do.

Cliff would not want me to list him in this exalted academic company. He is a builder, a man who picks up and feels a stone, judging from years of experience whether it is the right one for its place in the wall. This book comes to you from the building site not the ivory tower. He writes as he would speak to you over a mug of tea – directly, bluntly, sardonically, sadly, angrily, but passionately eloquently; and indeed often elegantly, for Cliff writes in the spirit of the old rural builder, within an innate understanding of the aesthetic of the word just as for the stone itself. He knows his stuff. He has read the books, studied the legislation, wrestled with the building regulations, argued with the planners and the politicians, cried out against the issuing of blanket advice which does not distinguish between solid stone and cavity walling. It is a call to arms.

Thomas Lloyd OBE FSA

Former Chair of the Historic Buildings Council for Wales
Author of "The Lost Houses of Wales"

INTRODUCTION

BY THEIR WORKS SHALL YE KNOW THEM

It is inevitable that any book which has the temerity to advise on subjects that are largely perceived as leaning heavily towards the personal is, at times, going to offend and outrage some readers. At other moments though, those same outraged may be seen to nod wisely and smile when the advice suits their own actions. It would be untrue to say that the idea is not to be provocative, and I am aware that it is a stance which will attract the bad opinion of some readers by hurting their feelings.

Writing books, especially with sincere motives, is not easy work. The decision to take such a stand is not to be made lightly if one has any sense at all, but in the case of my subject I feel the moment has arrived when such provocation is justified.

Many writers on these topics are so keen to avoid accusations of personal bias or dogma that their work can be full of carefully ambiguous generalisations, which soften the desired effect to a degree of political correctness that will render their advice virtually useless.

Those phrases like "in character" or "in keeping" do not give definite guidance. Most people know, or think they know, what is meant by "retaining the character" of an old building. The most obtuse individual will have a vague awareness of an old building's visual merits, but what his eye will accept as suitable in the way of restoration or conversion work will make another grind his teeth and turn his face away. If the idea is to help readers in a straightforward way to avoid losing the character of an old building whilst conserving its physical integrity, then blurring issues or hedging bets is not an option.

Some will think this arrogance, but others will see it as honesty. The fear of analysing, mentally testing and questioning the reasons why we like or dislike what we see is the real pity. If such matters are removed from debate it becomes virtually impossible to learn anything new or to develop our abilities.

I do not believe there are many who have lived in the seductively atmospheric surrounding of an old building, who will strongly disagree with most of the content of this book. The practical implementations of the advice however will cause some to shy at the prospect of change, even though that change may be fundamental to conserving their building for future generations.

We are at a crossroads on the route to better understanding our historic buildings. Issues of "sustainability" have forced those that regulate the construction industry to peer at the implications of historic building conservation with more attention than ever before. However, having generally paid that sector no more than lip service until present, now, under the fierce pressure of carbon

Panteg
A charming old house is turned, over the years, into what looks like an example of 1950s council housing *(picture courtesy of Tim Tagg)*.

reduction targets, their learning curve is a steep one and they are in danger of making decisions that could be severely detrimental to our historic buildings. Although they have been largely ignorant in their regulation to date, my hope was that the pressure for change might bring about a better future for that huge minority of our pre-1919 solid wall homes. One third of our entire housing stock in Wales. It seems that my hopes, although not entirely dashed, will not be met at anything like the level we conservators of historic buildings have wished for.

Conservation of historic buildings is, in general, seen by government as a side show in the construction industry. Any lobbying for better regulation is undertaken by comparatively small concerned groups, rather than by the product led, financially powerful organisations that have the clout to influence the direction of any new steps proposed. That direction will usually be biased toward the increased use of whatever products are provided by those financially powerful organisations.

The significance of the true and increasing value of the historic sector in this time of change has yet to be seen and properly acknowledged by those in power, and although I make this comment within a Welsh context it is applicable throughout the British Isles. Therefore the more people that become aware of the dangerous implications of proposed changes in the "official" attitude to our built heritage, the more likely will become a strong "unofficial" attitude to counter it.

On a more personal level, everyone is delighted when other people enjoy what we enjoy and to contemplate the idea that future generations could miss out on such a basic source of happiness holds no joy whatsoever.

Yet every time an old building becomes "ripe for renovation", which usually means the stripping out of interiors and often drastic plastic surgery to the exteriors, the perpetrators are denying themselves and other people a great deal of pleasure. Such shallow reaction turns these buildings into media influenced stage-sets, rather than the real settings they should be. Settings in which, as we live, work, love, nurture the young, grow old and sometimes die, we add our share of atmosphere to the amalgam of atmospheres implanted by previous generations. It is in this awareness that those settings can be felt to function properly, both in terms of their structures, and our sensibilities.

To conserve a legacy which the skill, energy, taste and wit of our forebears has provided should, in my strong opinion, only be regarded as admirable. Although this may involve us in a good deal of hard work and expense, there is clear benefit in the delight that comes with that involvement – in the sure knowledge that, by the use of the right materials, this house, this home, this valuable legacy, is able to continue into the future, becoming as much a legacy of our own as of those who went before us.

"By their works shall ye know them."

We can all choose how we shall be known. Spoilers by default, or conservators by choice.

ONE
IMPERFECT SOLUTIONS

In my previous book, "Precious Inheritance", I attempted to describe the importance of traditional materials in the repair and conservation of old buildings that are of solid wall construction. In particular the use of lime, which I consider to be the fundamental material in any attempt to alleviate inappropriate water retention and reverse the currently almost universal accelerated decay that has been inflicted upon the precious inheritance of that title. Not the high profile, grand, landscape changing buildings that seize the attention and therefore the lion's share of any grant funding available, but the ordinary historic home that is still lived in by real people.

One third of our housing stock in Wales is of solid wall construction. That amounts to almost half a million homes which are malfunctioning because of material ignorance – official, professional and amateur ignorance. That malfunction creates conditions that make these buildings more expensive to heat, both in financial and environmental terms. Combine those facts with the acceleration of decay caused by this lack of understanding, and what we have are nearly half a million homes that are unnecessarily unsustainable.

The basic difference in function between a cavity wall, a form of construction that has been around in mainstream building since 1919, (therefore, for less than 95 years at the time of writing) and the solid wall, which has been present in the British Isles for at least 2,000 years, is worth highlighting once again. Grasping the fact that there is a difference, and recognising what that difference is, brings everything into focus.

It is the initial moment of understanding, from which all truly successful building conservation springs. It is a remarkably easy concept to grasp and yet I have met people throughout my career who have strongly resisted that understanding, because to accept it would mean they are admitting to having done the wrong thing for years. Many would rather continue to do the wrong thing for the sake of their pride.

Functional
A solid wall works by absorption and evaporation (*drawing courtesy of Marianne Suhr*).

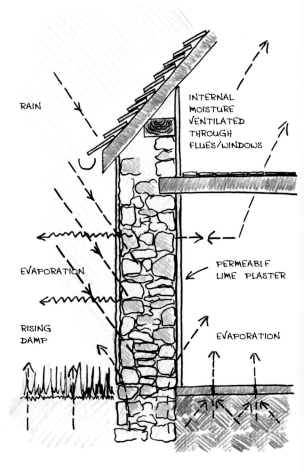

RAIN

INTERNAL MOISTURE VENTILATED THROUGH FLUES/WINDOWS

EVAPORATION

PERMEABLE LIME PLASTER

RISING DAMP

EVAPORATION

Shunned

(top) In rural areas, old cottages and farmhouses were abandoned in their thousands. *(bottom)* Abandoned farmhouse and new bungalow. In this case the house has a second life as a useful farm building.

That is wilfully destructive ignorance.

The modern cavity wall is designed to be waterproof in the modern sense. It is meant to shed water from its exterior surface and every attempt is made to ensure that function. Materials such as cement and oil or plastic based paints have been employed during the latter years of the roughly nine decades of the cavity wall's mainstream existence, to enhance that water shedding function.

The main purpose of the cavity was originally as a back-up system, that allowed for any leakage that may occur in the outer wall, to be drained away at the foot of the cavity and thus ensure that moisture did not reach the inside surface of the inner wall. Damp-proof courses and membranes are employed in this form of construction to further facilitate this method of "waterproofing".

The solid wall – the pre-1919 historic wall – and the rubblestone wall in particular, was never designed to be waterproof in the same sense as the later cavity wall. It was designed to allow water penetration to its much thicker profile than that of the cavity, absorbing that moisture into its traditional stone, earth and lime mortar construction until the rain stopped and the moisture content of the air outside the wall became less than that within. It then allowed the moisture to leave through the wall's surface by the process of evaporation. Those traditional materials that the historic building is constructed with, especially the lime content, are vapour permeable and thus allow this extremely effective process to happen.

It works in the same way that wet washing on a clothes line dries. If there is a breeze to help then it is obviously more effective. This is how pre-1919 solid wall structures keep the interiors of the building that they encompass dry.

For at least the last six decades, official understanding of that process has been virtually nil. Modern materials have been inflicted on these buildings by well meaning council-grant systems, building regulations and thus householders themselves, whenever repairs or maintenance were required. None of those modern materials are vapour permeable and therefore the way that these walls were designed to function has been routinely compromised for at least 60 years.

The result of this official material and functional ignorance has been the accelerated decay, and in some cases the virtual destruction, of swathes of our built heritage.

The 1960s and 70s were an especially destructive era for our traditional buildings. Public perception of the value of our built heritage was at an all-time low during those decades. The material abuse of old houses had already affected the performance of many, a fact which, combined with a general rise in living standards, created a culture that shunned the old traditional home. In rural areas, old cottages and farmhouses were abandoned or demolished by their thousands in favour of the modern, higher status bungalow. This happened all over the British Isles but was particularly evident in the Celtic homelands – Scotland, Ireland and of course Wales.

Ironically, the comparative rural poverty of these areas had initially acted as a preservative for these old houses – no money, no change – but once the affordability of modernity became more general, living in such a home lowered the status of the inhabitant. This attitude has gradually come full-circle in the last thirty years, and today living in an old house, or at least the current image of an old house – modernity with "original features" – has bestowed heightened status once again.

On a less dramatic but equally concerning note, thousands of these pre-1919 homes have, through material abuse, become damp, mould-ridden environments that have compromised the health of their inhabitants, and all this has been condoned by official policy.

The cessation of the ability of these walls to breathe and therefore maintain their own equitable balance of moisture leads to a build up of water within the structure, that decays any wooden elements within or against the wall (joists, lintels, skirting boards, floor-boards, door and window frames) and can and will decay the very stonework of the building, if that stone is porous and/or soft (some sandstones, limestones and slates for example). Considering the age already achieved by most of these buildings, accelerating their decay is an appallingly unsustainable act.

The water trapped in the walls also becomes cold in the winter, which cools their interior surfaces and causes, not only condensation, (which provides ideal conditions for mould growth) but requires the householder to burn more fuel to heat his home. It is worth repeating that this is bad for his pocket and bad for the environment. Combined with the decay, this makes a potential half-a-million existing homes in Wales unsustainable buildings and unhealthy environments for those that live in them.

Since the massive issue of global warming has arisen, with all its implications for the future of mankind, multiple counter-measures to those

Disfunctional

Absorption and evaporation is disrupted by the use of vapour impermeable materials – a cavity is designed to be 'water proof' and inflicting that thinking on solid walls causes malfunction and decay (*drawing courtesy of Marianne Suhr*).

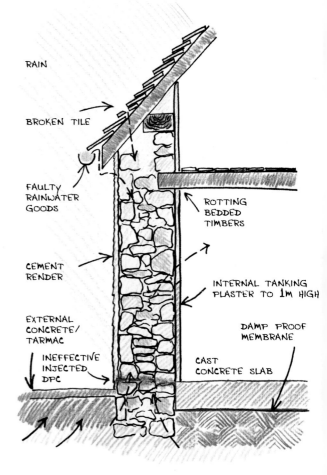

RAIN

BROKEN TILE

FAULTY RAINWATER GOODS

ROTTING BEDDED TIMBERS

CEMENT RENDER

INTERNAL TANKING PLASTER TO 1M HIGH

EXTERNAL CONCRETE/ TARMAC

DAMP PROOF MEMBRANE

INEFFECTIVE INJECTED DPC

CAST CONCRETE SLAB

CONCENTRATED GROUND MOISTURE

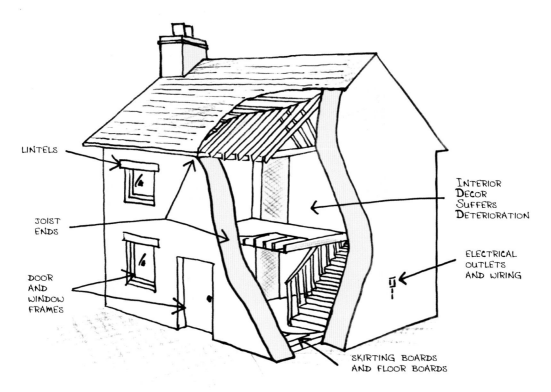

LINTELS

JOIST
ENDS

DOOR
AND
WINDOW
FRAMES

INTERIOR
DECOR
SUFFERS
DETERIORATION

ELECTRICAL
OUTLETS
AND WIRING

SKIRTING BOARDS
AND FLOOR BOARDS

Unable to breath

'Exploded' view of house façade
showing where rot strikes: joist ends,
window and door frames, lintels, floor
and skirting boards, and electrical wiring
and power points; water trapped in solid
walls by modern vapour impermeable
materials (principally cement and plastic
based masonry paints) will rot anything
vulnerable to moisture ingress –
including the very stone of the walls, in
some cases.

implications have been hurriedly distilled to a single word. Sustainability.

It is therefore a word of gigantic significance and the facets of that significance are legion. There is almost no area of life where "sustainability" does not apply in some form and at present there is confusion of implication and counter-implication, of hasty statement and action that is sometimes only partially researched and will undoubtedly result in some regrettable and avoidable mistakes. It is because of the huge pressure to rapidly find answers that can only really be discovered and implemented by sweeping changes in cultural attitudes, throughout the world, that unworkable policy decisions are being and will be made.

That pressure, especially carbon reduction targets, has resulted in some very ill-considered potential for regulation within the construction industry. Compromises that are of dubious merit and that, in some cases, will achieve the opposite of the desired effect are being disseminated as "sustainability" and may thus be enforced as regulation.

One result is that the cavity in modern construction must now be filled with insulation. A very few years ago that would have been considered ridiculous and any Building Regulations Officer would have been appalled at the perceived risk of "bridging", i.e. any water penetration to the outer wall of the cavity could track across the insulation and reach the inner wall. Now because of the drive to save energy by improving the performance of a house by preventing heat loss through the comparatively narrow cross-section of a modern cavity wall, those previous objections are ignored, even though the risks they represent are still relevant.

Placing insulation within a cavity wall will help to reduce heat loss, as long as that insulation is not compromised. However the chances of compromise are by no means slight.

If there is any water penetration to the outer wall (cracked render, poorly maintained paintwork, poor workmanship) and the insulation material is not entirely water-shedding, and many are not, the insulation in the cavity can become wet. That moisture will do two things. If the insulation touches the inner wall at any point, it will transfer damp to the inside of the house, and perhaps what is worse, wet insulation becomes cold in winter weather and ceases to insulate – in fact it could actually cool the house, thus achieving the opposite of the desired effect.

These problems are already becoming alarmingly apparent in buildings that are in exposed locations such as coasts and highlands and in some older cavity walls that are less robust than more modern examples.

The other consideration that is largely ignored in the race to insulate everything, is the fact that nearly all mainstream insulating materials are polluting in both their manufacture and in their disposal.

Most are by-products of the oil industry and therefore should already be considered dangerously finite and reliant on dwindling reserves that require high energy solutions to even access – a reliance that has been a root cause for the dilemma that the world faces today.

Their perceived effectiveness in alleviating global warming is therefore compromised at both ends of their lives. Embodied energy, with its own implications is being largely ignored and certainly not being drawn to the attention of the buying public.

I do not say, that given the time limits set for those carbon reduction targets and a fierce remit to create a policy which demonstrates immediate activity, that any alternative to cavity insulation is viable as yet. My intention is to point out that these circumstances have given little enough time for creative thought among those responsible within their comfort-zone, let alone outside it.

If those that regulate have created such an imperfect solution for a form of construction that they understand, how can we believe that they are able to provide effective answers to the same problem in a form of construction which functions in a way that has patently been ignored and misunderstood by those "authorities" for decades?

This "insulate and be damned" policy is, as I write, horrifyingly about to be inflicted on our older, solid-walled housing in the same spirit of ignorance that has coloured official attitudes to the functional ability of the solid wall ever since the Second World War.

This extraordinarily simple-minded, knee-jerk reaction to energy conservation is, at present, being government funded and actually carried out on pre-1919 solid wall structures on the surfaces of walls that are designed to "breathe".

If this policy is to have any positive effect at all on older buildings, then the walls of those buildings must first be dried out of accumulated moisture. They then must be made totally immune to further water penetration, and so will be inflicted with the whole arsenal of modern "waterproofing" materials. Those materials will, in the vast majority of cases, include cement as pointing or render.

The rigidity of cement makes it an appropriate material for use on modern buildings, with deep foundations that are designed to stop any structural movement.

The vast majority of old houses however, have little or nothing in the way of foundations. They are built straight onto the earth and are therefore subject to movement that cement's rigidity cannot accommodate. The cement will crack. Any stroll along a street bordered by pre-1919 buildings that are "cemented up" (which is most of them) will provide visual evidence of cracked render or broken pointing on the majority of the visible façades – often in the areas between one storey and the next – running from the cill of the upper window to the head of a lower, a relatively weak area of any mortar-bound construction.

Those are the visible areas that allow water penetration. Meanwhile, out of sight, with direct contact to any moisture in the ground beneath them, they will still be subject to rising damp, even if the inappropriate "waterproofing" materials covering their walls are always entirely uncompromised.

Cemented up
However well maintained, the cement will crack, often between one storey and the next.

To counter that threat, there will be the usual modern approach to rising damp. The injected chemical damp-proof course. A chemical damp-proof course needs to present an unbroken waterproof barrier from the outer to the inner edge of the wall. Within a wall of anything from half a metre to over a metre thick, built of rubblestone laid in a lime/earth mix and containing voids within that structure, this is simply not going to happen. It is a waste of money and effort to attempt to inject a silicone based viscous liquid into such a structure and expect it to prevent rising damp.

So the solid wall and its function is once again being misunderstood by the regulators and policy-makers. Placing insulation over the surfaces of these walls will simply add to their dysfunction. It will, whatever available insulating material currently on the mass market is used, inhibit the wall's ability to evaporate moisture and will therefore contribute to an even greater build up of water in the wall, increasing the acceleration of decay and lowering the temperature within the wall itself.

There have been attempts to develop breathable insulation materials, so that some of the designed function of the wall may be able to operate. Lime and hemp mixes have been proffered as sensible and environmentally friendly, but to date research into the insulation values of these mixes is inconclusive and they are unlikely at present to prove a market-leader. This is especially so as it is being researched by the concerned conservation sector in the face of much more powerful interested parties in the commercial insulation industry. It is a material, however, with high future potential.

Before this damaging, badly thought through process is inflicted on our pre-1919 buildings throughout the country, those interests behind this proposed policy should consider the obvious efficacy of returning the designed function of these walls to what once was, and should be, the norm.

Allow them to function as they are designed to function, regulating their own water content through the actions of absorption and evaporation, and finding their own equitable balance of moisture. Thus strongly contributing to a significant increase in their energy efficiency, before even thinking of wrapping them up in any material that is likely to actually decrease their ability to utilise their considerable thermal mass.

The aesthetic impact of exterior insulation on the old buildings in our communities would be massive. Uniform changes to the façades of a variety of individually distinct historic styles, recognisable signatures of their localities and the history of those areas, would turn our historic urban and rural landscapes into a blandness that denies the past. It is the latest in a series of ill-considered actions by "authority" to damage, often severely, both the visual appearance and the potential longevity of our pre-1919 buildings.

The well-meaning but materially flawed council grant system, thoughtless building regulation and now insulation, insulation, insulation. As ever, so far,

Cement pointing
This will cause damage on a lime
bounded brick wall by inhibition of
evaporation through the mortar joints –
cement's rigidity can prevent natural
movement, causing even stone to break.

with those that regulate within the historic sector, it is one step forward and one
back – ill-judged rules that create stasis. That is not progress.

The money would have been far better spent on subsidising the removal of
vapour impermeable materials from the outside walls of these buildings, and
the replacement of those materials with traditional breathable lime mortars,
renders or roughcasts. At present they malfunction because of material
ignorance and to contribute further to that malfunction seems close to idiotic.

I am aware that it is unrealistic to expect such a major shift in attitudes so
entrenched, and that the vast majority of those almost half a million pre-1919
solid-walled homes are in a state of malfunction and are likely to remain that
way until the knowledge of such a ridiculous situation, and the methods
required to correct it, becomes general.

At present it is very specialised knowledge and raising public awareness has
been an obsession of mine for many years.

Progress has been made – more and more people are becoming aware of both
the implications of current practice and the role that traditional, vapour
permeable materials can play in correcting the destructive and unsustainable
results of that practice, but there is still a long, long way to go.

"Precious Inheritance" contains much the same message, and this book I
hope, will play its part in continuing to broadcast these undeniable but largely
ignored facts. At the same time I intend to indulge in an aspect of that message,
the sheer physical beauty that can be achieved by the use of entirely appropriate
traditional materials, creating the right combination of texture, colour, shape,
dimension and proportion that is all the more pleasurable and satisfying because
in its very creation it is an act of conservation.

At present a huge part of the value that this legacy of former generations
represents, its direct connection to the past and a sense of human continuity, is
being visually disrupted to a degree that obscures and even denies any
awareness of age.

TWO

UNCOORDINATED CHAOS
AND COMMERCIAL HYPOCRISY

Herewith is reproduced a targeted letter, dated September 2011, that declares itself to be a Welsh Government funded programme, managed by British Gas and supported by the Energy Saving Trust (which is a material sub-contractor of British Gas).

Dear Homeowner

We are writing to you on behalf of the Welsh Government because it's likely that you live in a solid wall property, which means you may be eligible for the Welsh Government's Nest scheme. Nest is a programme that's designed to make Welsh homes warmer and more fuel efficient places to live. Homes that are hard to heat waste energy. Wasting energy means paying higher fuel bills.

You may be eligible to receive solid wall insulation at no cost if you: own or privately rent your home and; live in a home that's not energy efficient (F or G rated); and you or someone you live with is on a means tested benefit.

Insulating your solid walls can reduce heat loss by nearly half and save you around £375 a year on energy bills.

Whether you live in a solid wall property or not, other improvements which may be available through the scheme could include a new central heating boiler, loft insulation, cavity wall insulation, draught proofing for doors and windows and renewable energy technologies such as solar panels.

Your sincerely, The Nest team

This document offers funding to householders, who live in solid-walled homes, to insulate both the interiors and the exteriors of those walls.

On page two of the document the statement is made, unequivocally, that "solid walls allow more heat to pass through them than cavity walls". This statement is ambiguous at the very best and I would view it as largely untrue and therefore very misleading. Most of the rest of the information contained on that page would have difficulty surviving close scrutiny.

Solid wall insulation – frequently asked questions

1. Why insulate your solid walls?

Solid wall insulation can help you stop wasting energy and money. In winter, a well insulated house keeps the warmth in, so insulating your solid walls will help to heat your home more efficiently meaning that you stop wasting money on your energy bills.

2. Solid wall insulation – what's it all about?

If your home is made of brick or stone and was built before the 1920s, it's likely to have solid walls. Solid walls allow more heat to pass through them than through cavity walls. In fact, twice as much heat can be lost through an un-insulated solid wall as through an un-insulated cavity wall. This means that you end up paying more to keep your home warm. The good news is that solid walls can be insulated in two different ways: Internal insulation (inside) External insulation (outside)

3. How does solid wall insulation work?

Heat will always flow from a warm area to a cold one. In winter, the colder it is outside, the faster heat from your home will escape into the surrounding air. Solid wall insulation slows down the rate at which heat escapes, keeping as much of it as possible inside your home for as long as possible. Insulation works by coating the walls with a layer of material that only allows heat to pass through it very slowly meaning that your home stays warmer for longer, saving you money on your fuel bills.

In a survey published by British Gas in 2006, and carried out by IRT Surveys (highlighted on page 21 of "Precious Inheritance") it was found that older properties that had thermal mass, specifically mentioned as thick walls, i.e. solid-walled structures, outperformed cavity walls by some considerable margin – solid walls leaking as little as ten cubic metres of air per hour and cavity walls leaking as much as 23.6 cubic metres.

Still, not many members of the public saw or were aware of that report and nor it seems was British Gas for they have completely reversed that verdict in this document. The 2006 survey was noticed by some however, and it prompted Hank Dittmar, Chief Executive of the Prince's Foundation for the Built Environment to comment that "wind turbines, solar panels and other high-tech green devices may get the media attention, but the smartest way to save energy may be to live in a Tudor house and insulate the attic and repair the windows". No mistaking his interpretation.

Another study was published in 2007 entitled Age Energy Research (a study of energy usage of buildings relative to their age), supervised by the Departmental Architect of HMCS Estates, the Ministry of Justice. With strong support from English Heritage and the Building Research Establishment, it determined energy use within the broad range of buildings owned by the Ministry throughout the UK with a view to decreasing that energy use. Its findings were specific. "The oldest buildings (pre-1900) use the lowest energy by a margin of 13% compared to their nearest competitor, buildings from 1900-1939," (he wasn't looking at solid versus cavity, but age determines structure). The architect's recommendations for energy conservation included the following:

"Buildings built pre-1900 should be prioritised for retention in the portfolio," and "Buildings of the 1940s, 1950s and 1960s should be prioritised for disposal".

So what's going on?

In the light of this Welsh Government initiative, I feel that some of the content of an "engagement workshop", held in 2012 to discuss a forthcoming CADW/BRE publication will be of interest.

The proposed publication is intended to deliver guidance on energy conservation in the historic sector, with advice on "risk assessment, pointers to other research and examples of good practice". The workshop was also intended to look at how "Balancing carbon reduction and preserving heritage" would "feed into Building Regulations". I was present (and active) at that meeting.

The workshop was addressed by the representative of the Building Research Establishment, seconded to the Welsh Government as an advisor. Building Regulations have devolved from Westminster to Cardiff, so Wales will have their own set by the end of 2013, and BRE involvement was required in all areas of the new regulations. The BRE representative stated categorically that research so far had shown that any form of insulation on the inside surface of a solid wall inhibited its function and, because of the implications that had for insulative failure, interior surface insulation for historic walls should not be employed (compare to statement two on page two of the Nyth letter).

Furthermore, the research had not reached a stage that would define the result of insulating the outside of those walls, but as the inside had negative results and the publication had a deadline, they had no choice but to recommend that exterior surfaces be insulated.

When pressed, the BRE representative admitted that their recommendations were based on incomplete research and that they had no true idea of the consequences and that this could lead to negative results.

In response to further questioning it was also stated that the BRE was aware that the software employed to calculate energy performance was written entirely for modern structures, but used nonetheless to calculate performance in all buildings, including the half a million historic, solid-walled homes in Wales.

As there was no intention of implementing new software (too expensive, too much new training required), then calculations would continue to be made, and decisions about performance and insulative requirements reached, using the existing software.

It was also admitted, that BRE was aware that most solid-walled homes, benefitting from thermal mass supplied by thick walls, already performed better than their cavity equivalents and therefore all judgements on energy conservation in these old buildings were being based on false readings that indicated a lower level of performance that was in fact the case. A lime bonded wall that is dry can have an insulation value as low as 0.9, whereas most modern assessments assume a value of 2.5 for a mass wall (Historic Scotland – INFORM 2008).

In spite of all this, the proposed document would advise that pre-1919 buildings should have additions made to their outside surfaces that will alter their aspect and visual historical relevance. This decision is based on incomplete research, has potentially disastrous consequences for energy performance and could increase acceleration of decay. The advice to implement these acts on individual historic structures would be based on performance figures that were knowingly wrong.

The Welsh Government, by the admission of its own advisors, does not seem to know what it is doing, and since the BRE is a UK wide organisation, no doubt its recommendations will apply beyond Wales' borders.

Does the word farcical spring to mind? So, we have statements in the Nyth document in 2011, a Welsh Government funded programme, contradicted by earlier research from British Gas in 2006, who are the managers of that Nyth initiative. Contradicted also by research from the Ministry of Justice in 2007 and by current research from BRE, who advise unequivocally that insulating the interiors of solid walls – as offered, even recommended by Nyth at the taxpayer's expense – can be harmful to those buildings. Why are the Welsh Government willing to allow manipulation of this kind to overrule solid evidence? Are they being seriously remiss, or is there some other agenda? Who benefits in all this?

It seems to me that the manufacturers, distributors and installers of insulation products are the beneficiaries, while the unfortunate historic homeowner and his house are likely to be the victims of acts that, at best, could be useless and at worst will be actually harmful.

How many homes with solid walls have already taken up the offer? And in the light of the uncoordinated chaos of false advice and dubious action, should those homeowners not have the opportunity to reverse those actions – once again at the taxpayer's expense?

It is further food for thought that the solid-walled structures used in both the British Gas and the Ministry of Justice's studies will almost certainly be examples that are materially abused, for the simple reason that unless every one was a listed building, they are unlikely to have had their natural function restored by the use of lime mortars, renders and washes. Even if each was listed, there is an overwhelming likelihood that cement and plastic paints predominated.

Those buildings were almost certainly already malfunctioning, and yet their performance is shown to outstrip the cavity-walled examples. Think how much better they would have performed if each was balancing the moisture content within its walls by absorption and evaporation, as they were designed to do. The contrast would have been even greater.

Hank Dittmar's comments about repairing windows and insulating the attic may sound slightly tongue-in-cheek, but are in fact astoundingly relevant, both to the visual appearance of an old building and its energy performance. Insulating the attic space of an old house is entirely sensible to prevent the loss of rising heat, but to insulate the walls of such buildings will be destructive to both their aesthetic and their function.

Keeping older properties in use is as important as some of the newer carbon reduction programmes. Once returned to their natural function by the use of vapour permeable traditional materials, properly maintained, traditionally built structures will last for hundreds of years, and can play a full part in managing our carbon expenditure now and long into the future.

THREE
AGE CONCERN

Our cities, towns, villages and rural areas have many old, pre-1919 buildings on which visual disruption has been achieved by a combination of hideous alterations that contrive to "straighten up" these homes and turn them into "modernised" versions of their former selves. This has been done by the removal of early details such as doors and windows, and their replacement with unsuitable substitutes, often scrambling almost all semblance of their age in the process.

The exterior finishes on these abused houses are almost invariably modern. Cement renders and pebble-dash, frequently covered in plastic based masonry paints. Corners and edges brought to rigid, sharp angles. Any hint of bulge or lean ironed out to please the sensibilities of an owner and, sadly, a general population that subscribes to such actions because their knowledge, understanding and appreciation of the beauty of age in a building is virtually non-existent.

Admittedly the lack of understanding is not entirely the fault of that population. A visual architectural culture that has developed over the last 150 years into the obsession with "modernisation", that culminates currently in a plethora of TV programmes that serve the British preoccupation with home-ownership, and the financial value of that ownership.

The viewer of both the programmes and the actual properties is, at present, the victim of attitudes that have grown and developed socially around the essentially urban views of what it is that makes an "old" house desirable and increases its monetary value.

These views have grown from the rich mulch of the perceived status and kudos achieved by fulfilling the precepts demanded by fashion's dictates, and

Modern exteriors
(left) Grim and grey pebble-dash and *(below)* masonry painted cement render.

Ripe for renovation
The stimulus for much ruination.

thus impressing fellow fashion followers. However as is the case with most popular fashion, what is fashionable is dictated not by those who fall under its spell, but by those who create it for their own reward. Fashion is product led.

These views even have their own language. A language that has become such a collection of clichés that their true meaning is often substantially obscured and they simply become sounds, signals to the "property-watcher" that those comments relate to an "old" house, and that house comes with status attached.

The jargon includes those estate agents' old familiars, "original features", "exposed beams" and perhaps less immediately desirable, but nonetheless still dripping with potential, "ripe for renovation".

Every one of those noises is either a misnomer or has the potential to cause further damage to an old property, that is already likely to have been visually compromised.

"Original features" usually means that there is something old in the house that miraculously survives. To term such a survival original can only be spurious. How can the estate agent know that this thing is original? It may be old, even historic – but original?

The word "features" itself has come to mean anything that even suggests age in a building, and has now been turned from noun to quasi-adjective, as in "feature property".

"Exposed beams" usually means that there are joists, rafters or purlins that are not concealed by a ceiling. In most cases, if not painted black, it is de rigueur to strip, stain and varnish them, as is true of almost any piece of visible timber in the house – all of it surrounded by the flat aesthetic of modern plasterboard and vinyl paints.

The reader may think this view pedantic, but such inaccurate terminology has become the carrot that tempts those for whom "ripe for renovation" holds a strong attraction.

"Ripe for renovation" is a phrase that has been the stimulus for much ruination. The removal of genuine historic details from old houses and the infliction of suburban rectitude on buildings that really do not deserve it, and will consequently suffer from the material ignorance that such "ripeness" encourages, often causing substantial acceleration of decay to the actual structure.

If this is not a reason for concern then it really should be.

If you know that certain everyday actions can and do actually reduce the performance of your property as a shelter and shorten its lifespan, why would you cause them to be carried out? Just to satisfy your own received image of what an old house should be?

Alarmingly, the lack of knowledge that causes such harm is not restricted to estate agents and their customers. Mortgage providers that employ surveyors to assess the condition of a property before they will lend money against the security of that property have, to date, shown that the irresponsibility of the industry stretches beyond simple, recession causing greed, and into the realm of inflicting conditional damage to people's homes.

The vast majority of all construction industry professionals – architects, surveyors and engineers (although, there are a few outstanding examples) – will have very limited knowledge of the structure and function of the pre-1919 solid-walled building, as none of these professions require that knowledge to achieve their qualifications. The combination of surveyors, with little or no knowledge of how solid-walled buildings function, and mortgage providers, that impose conditions on those loans that are entirely based on judgements made by those professionals, leads to acts that will damage such a building.

Cement concrete floor slabs with plastic damp-proof membranes and injected chemical damp-proof courses, are two such common conditions imposed on what the average surveyor perceives as "a damp, old house", internal waterproof cement "tanking" is another. Viable "cures" for a cavity-walled structure. All these acts can and will cause increased damp problems and accelerate the decay of the majority of pre-1919 structures.

So the purchaser gets his loan, causing damage to his property to achieve it, and the lender has, as security for that loan, a property in worse condition than before his terms were met, and one that will not last as long as it should. It is a cycle of stupidity and everyone is a loser.

There will, eventually, be a fundamental shift in attitudes and material use and there are signs of approaching enlightenment. For the first time in the many years that I have been involved in the lime revival, we are finding that some surveyors are recommending action by "contractors who understand the function of solid walls and have had experience in alleviating damp by the use of traditional materials and methods".

The recommendations always used to be to contact damp-proofing companies who would mess up your old house, adding more cement, tanking materials and chemicals to the mix which might hide the damp until the guarantee runs out, but will not cure it.

Lately, we have successfully represented house purchasers, writing reports that counter the mortgage providers' surveys and recommendations and which strongly advocate traditional methods that revive the correct function of the old house in question and eliminate damp without the use of damaging materials and chemicals. So there is a slowly growing recognition, that a house which functions correctly because lime mortars, renders, plasters and washes have been used, is going to last longer, be healthier to live in and have fewer problems than one that is cemented up, covered with plastic paint and rotting away faster than it should. This will eventually result in the correctly limed old house having a higher value than its cement covered counterpart. We will, in the not too distant future, hear new "estate agent speak" such as "benefits from a lime render and no damp-proof course". Roll on that day, for it will indicate a massive improvement in the attitude to conservation of our built heritage, an increase in the energy performance for such houses and a decrease in financial outlay to heat them, with the consequent decrease in fuel consumption and carbon dioxide pollution. A cycle of enlightenment where everyone wins.

Until then, we conservators who are called in to help improve living conditions within old houses (often as a last resort) will continue to be the bearers of bad news.

Frequently it is glaringly obvious that the householder has spent a great deal of time, effort and money on doing entirely the wrong thing to their home, and the only answer is to reverse those harmful acts and begin again with the right materials. This is a concept that can be very difficult to face up to. Nobody likes to be told they are wrong and nobody likes the prospect of removing and undoing already completed, careful work. There has to be a change, a conversion of beliefs to produce the motivation required, and that can be a step too far for many.

The visual inappropriateness of modern, rigid, vapour impermeable materials

Imperfect imaginary vision
Cement pointed 'exposed stone' and fake cementitious 'wobbliness'.

on old houses seems sometimes to create a sub-conscious awareness in an owner that all is not as it should be. This can cause a striving to alleviate that uneasiness in some way, often creating a cartoon of the real thing in the process. "This house is so modernised that we need to do something to make it look old again." In our part of the world that something nearly always revolves around the word stone.

So fake cementitious wobbliness, wavy cement render patches, horribly imperfect imaginary visions of how, it is thought, an old house should look tend to predominate.

Nearly all those visual wince-inducers are designed to emphasise that the house is built of STONE. Even if that stone is covered in a cement render (to keep out the damp!) that render is often scribed and marked in a dreadful imitation of the stone beneath.

The vast majority of the populace live in homes that are built of cement blocks, or if they're lucky, bricks. The vast majority of those are rendered over with cement and painted with masonry paint, presenting that flat, monotonous finish synonymous with modern housing that is so ubiquitous that the eye hardly registers it any more. It is therefore relatively unusual to live in a stone built home. This rarity has a status value and so results in the determination, by some owners, that everyone should be made thoroughly aware of the stone in the construction. Hence the attempts at imitation when the stones are covered in cement.

Just as often though, it results in the exposed-stone building. Houses built of rubblestone (random, uncut stone), often a poor mixed medium, that was never intended by those that built them to be left uncovered, aware as they were of the vulnerability of much such stone to weather damage. When built, that stone was almost always covered with a protective lime-based finish.

Three lime coverings were employed historically – limewash straight onto the stone, a lime render or plaster, or a lime roughcast. Both the render and the roughcast would then also be finished with several coats of limewash.

These coverings protected often vulnerable stonework from weather damage, facilitated the intended function of absorption and evaporation and provided an aesthetic that cannot be matched by cement and plastic paint.

Removal of those traditional coverings returns the stone to a vulnerable state, and decreases the wall's efficiency in controlling moisture, which, in turn, often results in the use of cement render as that moisture control breaks down and damp appears on the invariably cemented up interior walls.

The drive to expose stone is frighteningly widespread, and some householders will actually put up with poor conditions within their home rather than lose the exposed stone look.

It is perhaps indicative of the historic facts that the word exposed is used in this context. If those walls had always been uncovered, then the use of the

The three traditional lime coverings
(above) Limewash straight onto lime-mortar pointed stone. *(middle)* Limewashed lime render. *(bottom, picture courtesy of Mike Thain)* Limewashed lime roughcast.

descriptive term exposed would be unnecessary. Only the poorest of dwellings, and those the most remote from a source of lime, would remain uncovered by the end of the 18th Century, and if the incumbent possessed the wherewithal and the opportunity then they too would have been limed.

I cannot count the times, when attempting to persuade a home owner to do the right thing, that I have heard in response, "Oh, but I like to the see the stone," strongly resisting the fact that they are ignoring potential deterioration of that stone and thus their house. What is meant by a great many of them, sometimes quite consciously, is "Oh, but I like other people to see the stone". It is only that witness by others that confers the kudos that a stone built home brings to its owner, and it is all based on a false premise.

My dream is, of course, that eventually that status will be transferred to owners of old homes who truly understand that the appliance of lime coverings and their practical function, combine to conserve their buildings, create comfortable, healthy homes, and a beauty that far outstrips the limited aesthetic of cement pointed exposed rubblestone. That would be status well deserved, as it is rooted in awareness and knowledge rather than denial and ignorance.

That dream is coming closer, as those confusing sustainability issues have highlighted figures that no one had bothered to investigate before. The fact that such a significant minority – one third of our housing stock – is of pre-1919 solid-walled structure. Although the proposed insulation farce has also been a result of those figures, there is a general move in organisations, such as Construction Skills (the national training and qualification body for the construction industry) towards an awareness, for the first time, of the need for different materials and the skills to use those materials on nearly half a million homes in Wales, and up to one sixth of the entire housing stock in England. Those figures do not include buildings that are not domestic dwellings, such as industrial structures, warehouses, ecclesiastical buildings and of course farm buildings, all of which have the potential to become domestic dwellings.

The survey behind those figures, published in 2005 by the National Heritage Training Group, itself a part of Construction Skills, highlights the chronic shortage of tradesmen with the understanding and ability to undertake works on these buildings without creating repeated damage to their designed function. It has instigated a qualification system, the HSS Card, which is achieved through the NVQ curriculum and is designed to indicate to employers and homeowners that the holder has adequate knowledge and skill to work successfully on pre-1919 solid-walled structures. At the time of writing English Heritage were indicating that works tendered by them would only be awarded to companies that had one third of its workforce thus carded.

Such official recognition, for the first time, that the problem actually exists is a step in the right direction, and quite a large step. Ten years ago, there was no such understanding within those organisations that influence the way works are specified and carried out in the historic sector of the industry, and a steady refusal to look the problem in the eye, until those sustainability issues raised the profile of the sector beyond the limited designations of listed buildings. This change in attitude will help to cause changes, eventually, in general perceptions of our old houses, as long as the dangerously retrograde official "insulation policy" doesn't destroy the initiative, and there is a very real possibility that it might.

It is still a struggle that requires energy and commitment to ensure that once understanding on a useful level is embedded, it will stay in place, and not be uprooted by the widespread lack of knowledge that feeds the general complacency that surrounds the subject.

Attempts by the National Heritage Training Group to implement "Training for Trainers", to deliver the required NVQ's, have proven patchy in their success so far, largely due to poor response from Further Education establishments, and of course the financial fall-out of the current economic recession that has slowed down so many initiatives.

In a more local context though, another positive result of the growing perception of the necessity to understand our old buildings and provide information, advice and education on the subject, has been the establishment in 2009 of the Tywi Centre at Llandeilo in Carmarthenshire. In "Precious Inheritance" I bemoaned the fact that although England and Scotland both had centres of excellence that dispensed that knowledge and training, Wales was sadly lacking. The private sector had for years been doing its best to take up the slack. For over a decade our own company, The Lime Company of West Wales (TLC) has provided courses covering a wide range of theory and practice in South West Wales, and teaching on SPAB and RICS courses, much further abroad. Ty Mawr Lime, near Brecon has been doing the same in Powys for even longer.

The Tywi Centre, originally an initiative by the National Trust, with strong involvement by those of us who were already acting as training providers, has developed over the last few years, into a well-funded equivalent of the English and Scottish centres. It provides a hub for a growing core of initiatives in the provision of education and training, specifically aimed at the conservation of our built heritage, rural skills and their direct connection to the conservation of our species on the planet. This combined with a new look set of Building Regulations here in Wales that will at least acknowledge that these old buildings exist, and exist in a different context to post-1919 buildings, are very positive moves in the right direction. Existing Building Regulations recognise historic buildings as those that are listed, or of some other specific historic interest, and make some provision for their continued existence within the regulations. Some officers were beginning to be persuaded that it was wise to consider looking at all structures that were built in exactly the same way and therefore required

Training and education
(above top) The author demonstrates lime pointing technique and *(above bottom)* the mixing, application and properties of limewash. *(below)* Practical participation is strongly encouraged. *(photos by Noreen Hollywood)*

The lime cycle

In a world full of oil-industry by-products – this is a stunningly green product *(drawing courtesy of Tŷ-Mawr Lime)*.

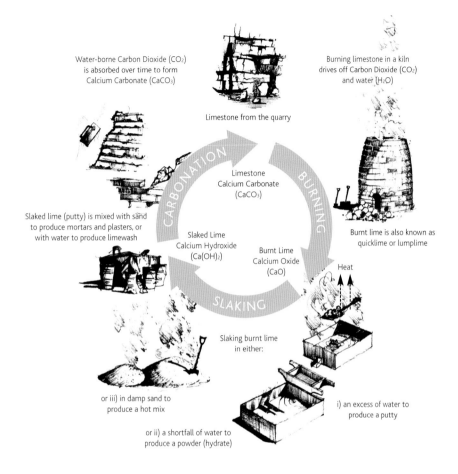

Water-borne Carbon Dioxide (CO_2) is absorbed over time to form Calcium Carbonate ($CaCO_3$)

Limestone from the quarry

Burning limestone in a kiln drives off Carbon Dioxide (CO_2) and water (H_2O)

CARBONATION

BURNING

Limestone Calcium Carbonate ($CaCO_3$)

Slaked lime (putty) is mixed with sand to produce mortars and plasters, or with water to produce limewash

Slaked Lime Calcium Hydroxide ($Ca(OH)_2$)

Burnt Lime Calcium Oxide (CaO)

Burnt lime is also known as quicklime or lumplime

Heat

SLAKING

Slaking burnt lime in either:

or iii) in damp sand to produce a hot mix

i) an excess of water to produce a putty

or ii) a shortfall of water to produce a powder (hydrate)

exactly the same treatment as those special few, in the same light, but that light needed directing, and most found it too complicated to consider, in any depth, the wisdom of "ticking" outside the box.

The new Building Regulations, set to come into force in 2013, are predominantly aimed at promoting carbon reduction targets within the construction industry as a whole. An intensely complicated and convoluted subject, that at present seems to be revolving around "insulation, insulation, insulation".

They are however, struggling with definitive rules of practice for the historic sector, a much simpler, straightforward area to deal with, if only they would grasp the nettle and actively promote positive material change on these old buildings. Take out the cement and put back the lime. Get the buildings working properly first then add the bolt-on goodies if necessary. Conservation of historic buildings and carbon reduction should and could be achieved in tandem.

Those acts, although admittedly a huge task nationwide, with all its training implications, will have an equally huge permanent and positive effect on the environment, and a workforce trained to carry out these skills will have a long-term future in ongoing repair and maintenance of that massive minority of our housing stock, using a material that can be produced at a low temperature industrially, thus minimising fuel use and its consequent waste gasses, and which "cures" when used, by re-absorbing carbon dioxide. Lime "carbonates" to bring it to a set, and will take back up to 25% of the CO_2 it produces in manufacture. In a world full of materials made from oil industry by-products that already have an horizon in sight, that are costly in terms of production pollution and fuel use, none of which re-absorb CO_2 at any stage of their existence; lime is a stunningly green product.

The use of lime as an energy performance enhancer in those half a million homes in Wales, and millions of other buildings throughout the UK, would be far more positive than poorly thought through, cheaply applied measures that may well, by the admission of the Government's advisers, prove to be counter-productive, and therefore short-term.

Of course it is much easier to succumb to lobbying groups supported by large companies that manufacture insulation materials that, in modern terms, are easy to understand and require minimal skill to install.

When, and if, the research into the question of the actual result of using modern insulation materials on the outside surfaces of pre-1919 solid-walled structures is complete, and it is shown to have detrimental effects on those buildings, will there be an admission of the facts? If by then thousands of homes have already been treated in this way, will that admission result in boom time for "insulation removers" in a government backed scheme to put things right?

What do you think?

My personal experience is of relevance to this part of the narrative. My own home, dating from at least the 17th Century, with additions and alterations in both the 18th and 19th Centuries, is as you may expect, of solid, rubblestone construction.

Built of Preseli Bluestone, the same that stands at Stonehenge, bedded in "prydd melin", earth mortar, leavened with lime, it received a "sentence of suffocation" in the late 1950s, when the council gave a grant to the then owners, to install a bathroom and flushing W.C. (forty years before we moved in).

Nothing wrong with that. A definite improvement over the tin bath and the outside tŷ-bach.

At the same time, however, it was decided to use that "magic" cement, to cover the entire building in hard, grey pebble-dash, thus "water-proofing" it. The house stands high in the Preseli Hills in south west Wales and has to withstand (and in fact, for over 350 years has withstood) Atlantic coastal weather. That can mean sideways rain for weeks on end.

Manmade vs natural
A mountain of chemically noxious insulation material that at the end of its life will become 'landfill'. Sheep's wool – natural and biodegradable.

Dolaumaen
From grim and grey and very damp
to lime roughcast and limewashed:
breathing, dry and healthy.

We lived in the house, in its "waterproof" coat for two years, before we were able to remove the cement and restore the correct function of absorption and evaporation to its walls, and so we were able to compare performance before and after.

The amount of water trapped in the walls was such that a gable end was found to be close to collapse when the cement was removed. A lime roughcast, with limewash of a colour that was found beneath, was reinstated, interior lime plaster repaired and renewed and the loft space insulated, not with high energy, manufactured chemical complexes, but with sheep's wool, that has gone through a minimal amount of technical interference to comply with fire resistance and to repel insect attack. It does not require manufactured energy to make it and at the end of its life, it biodegrades. It is every bit as efficient an insulator as the chemically noxious substances currently being pushed as green.

Then we waited while, with an almost audible sigh of relief, the house came back to life.

Within the first year of that experience the volume of fuel that was burnt by us during its years of malfunction was reduced by an eighth. Only solid fuel is used in this house, in a pre-war (1936 model) kitchen range and a woodburning stove, and the current usage of fuel has further reduced by half that amount again, as the retained water in the walls has evaporated and their natural function of moisture control has fully returned.

This means a considerably warmer house in winter and represents an 800kg saving in fuel consumption per annum.

If anyone was to suggest that I insulate the walls of this house, my refusal would be most forceful.

FOUR
CREATIVE DETERIORATION

I wrote in the previous chapters of the various cement and masonry paint repairs that are visually inappropriate on most pre-1919 buildings. There are, however, some finishes in these modern materials that demonstrate mind boggling creativity – albeit a creativity more attuned to the school of disastrous results than to any reality that may have ever graced some of those buildings during their existence to date.

The "let's pretend the cement render is stone" look has become wildly popular in spite of the fact that it always looks like the pretence. There are several forms of this look, among them the carefully crafted, indented, false mortar joints, tracing imaginary rubblestone shapes in the cement and the less ambitious, lumpy, wavy look achieved by varying the thickness of the cement render and forming random "hillocks" (sometimes with false mortar joints as well) in an attempt to create the impression that beneath each lump is a piece of real stone. This technique is so popular that in a sort of dot-dash Morse code look, it has caught on in new build lately as well.

Two ironies grin at each other through this fog of self-deception. These obvious, unusually ugly fakes are covering the real thing up in an attempt to stop damp penetration, and in doing so are actually encouraging water retention and accelerating the decay of the walls they cover.

Let's pretend the cement render is stone
(below) Dot-dash 'Morse code' look.
(bottom left) The lumpy wavy look.
(bottom right) Carefully crafted, indented, false mortar joints.

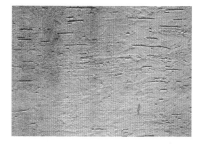

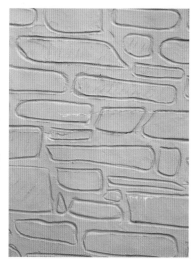

Another less common, but by no means less startling finish, is the "fish-scale" look. This takes the imitation of rubblestone to almost surreal heights. It can only be achieved with a good deal of effort, this careful shaping of cement render – to what end? An apparently overlapping series of raised "scale" like protrusions. No rubblestone wall ever looked remotely like this and yet there can be no doubt that the effect being striven for is its imitation.

When I first saw it I thought that it must be a one-off. The wild transference of this imagery onto a reality that has been completely lost in translation. But I was wrong. This finish is to be found dotted around south west Wales and unless it is all the work of a particular individual (a sort of cement render Banksy) and circumstances make that unlikely, then there is, or was, a school of very unreal fake stone finish out there following a curriculum that I fear may be based visually in the Early Artex Movement. Its creativity is not lost on me. The aesthetic it produces though, I can only see as one of the more extreme versions of the desire to shout "I live in a stone house!". Whatever this actually looks like, you know it's meant to represent rubblestone. The practical effect, however, is destructive in the long run.

The "Wavy Remnants" look is another way of expressing a perceived vision of the old rubblestone house. A wall with most of its surface exposed, pointed between the stones with hard, grey cement and with the added visual fillip of both large and small patches of cement render, often painted just to make sure that the eye cannot possibly skip over them, and to create maximum contrast with the exposed stone, often emplaced around windows and doors.

These cement render patches always have wavy edges, carefully contrived, I must assume, to imitate the imaginary remnants of an imaginary historic finish.

Imaginary historic finishes
(below left) The 'fish-scale' look is not a 'one-off'! *(below right)* The 'Wavy Remnants' look.

My imagination runs amok in its quest to interpret this vision of "how an old house must look" and the conclusion that seems most likely is that by creating those blobs on the surface of an otherwise exposed rubblestone wall, a film-set style of genteel ruination, that the apparent deterioration of the building, is the goal – although strangely belied by the often smart plastic paintwork and stylised, decorative cement pointing. Sometimes just the corners of the building, with their more visually impressive quoin stones are left exposed, giving the impression that

More 'Wavy Remnants'
Large and small patches of painted cement render, creating a wavy edged, 'film set' style of genteel ruination.

the render has fallen off to leave the surprise of rubblestone beneath.

These theatrical creations are, as in all these examples, designed to emphasise the exposed stone and the contrived image of deterioration is sadly prophetic, for as usual the materials used to create the effect will inhibit the function of the wall and accelerate its decay.

This effect is often striven for on internal walls as well, only it seems that it is best received by those who admire it if the visual situation is reversed. The wall mainly covered with painted cement render but a patch of stone left exposed within the wavy edge of the render surrounding it.

Sometimes, just the corners
The render has 'fallen off' the quoin stones.

The "stone-clad stone house" is possibly the ultimate irony achieved in the quest to make a solid rubblestone wall waterproof in the modern sense, to shed water from the outside surface of the wall in a bid to keep the interior damp free. It doesn't work of course, the stone-cladding is a cement based composite (known often as sticky stone) and attached to the wall using cement once again. Therefore any movement will open up cracks and allow water penetration, creating all the usual problems.

Stone-cladding looks like no natural stone that I know of and is usually parti-coloured, leaning towards the light shades associated with limestone but patently not limestone. Stone-cladding always looks like the fake that it is and never seems to fit the colour and texture of local stone, no matter where it is used.

So what moves people to stone-clad their old stone house? I assume that it is part of the same drive to impress stone on others, the drive that has created the Pretentious Cement Fakes, the Fish-Scale Look and the Wavy Remnants. However in this case it is a manufactured finished product designed to be used by people who live in modern brick or block built homes, often identical in

The stone-clad stone house
Possibly the ultimate irony.

shape and size, in an attempt at individuality, to make their home stand out from those surrounding it.

The creativity and often careful work that has gone into many of these misguided efforts are completely missing from the stone-clad solution. It is an easy, quick-fix that, if used on old houses, doesn't "do what it says on the tin". The one saving grace that I can think of is its chuckle value. Stone-cladding a stone house and expecting anyone to believe it is funny.

I wrote in my introduction about the phrases "in keeping" and "in character" and I have no doubt that all the above have, at their hearts, a partly formed but badly informed drive to achieve something of the sort.

All these images of old buildings have floated to the top of an architectural version of a "mess of pottage". A gently seething mix of false truths largely based on a Hollywood version of Ye Olde Britain that has created a form of received pronunciation throughout the last few generations and developed into a kind of pick and mix version of fake history that has had a long lasting effect on the choices many people make when they live in an old house – an historic home – both in aesthetic and vitally in material choice.

Do not mistake these criticisms for high-handed superiority. I have little doubt that the majority of those that treat their houses in these ways are content and even pleased with the visual results. My point is that with the right knowledge and attitude, the real thing can be achieved so easily and in many cases less expensively.

FIVE

'THE ANCIENT PRACTICE' AND ENDURING MYTH OF RUBBLE–WORSHIP

In 1887 William Morris founded the Society for the Protection of Ancient Buildings (SPAB), an organisation that has been fighting for the survival of our built heritage in the British Isles ever since.

In those first decades of its existence SPAB gained the nickname "The Anti-Scrape Society" because of its resistance to the removal of lime coverings from houses, a fashion brought about by a combination of factors, perhaps the strongest being a fast growing urban population. The generally revolting conditions experienced by those newly large urban populations caused them to mythologise the "cleaner, healthier and more natural" conditions of the country.

The "Rural Idyll" was born and grew into a wishful and strongly sentimental popular fashion that saw most things rustic as having a degree of purity that they did not actually possess. This included nature's building block – stone. Not the pollution covered "filthy brick" of the Victorian conurbation but "clean, healthy and natural stone". It had to be seen and so the practice of exposing stone began.

SPAB realised that this removal of lime shelter coats was not only the immediate destruction of something often beautiful (Ruskin especially espoused the visual qualities of lime coverings) but also something functional. The lime coverings were part of the ability of the solid wall to keep the interior of the building it encompassed dry. They had been used for this purpose for hundreds of years and it took but a few decades to devalue and destroy these lime coverings, and the result has echoed down the years to our time. Exposed stone has only been around as "the norm" for less than 150 years. Before the 1880s exposed stone was a rarity here in Wales and throughout most of the British Isles.

The Victorians loved the idea of exposed stone so much that they began new-builds designed specifically to look like rubblestone construction. Built of good stone, not the random quality of a real rubblestone building, the stone was roughed-up on its face to represent an undressed image of rustic simplicity. In fact this carefully contrived look was called "rusticated" stonework and being usually of specially chosen building stone, always laid in lime mortar, it did not require either the protection of a lime covering or that covering's assistance to achieve effective breathability. A cursory inspection of such construction will soon show the deceit for what it was – carefully cut stone often of different sizes to further the impression of randomness.

It all fitted in very well to the Victorian Gothic revival – a confident,

William Morris
Craftsman, poet, and socialist and founder of the Society for the Protection of Ancient Buildings *(picture courtesy of the RPS Collection at the NMeM/SSPL).*

Victorian stonework

(above) A non-conformist chapel, the façade in 'exposed' rubblestone – beautifully executed, effective and misleading. *(below)* 'Rusticated' stonework, carefully contrived to look like rubblestone construction.

extravagant, imaginary reinvention of mediaeval Britain. This imaginary Britain from an idealised past was, of course, largely an exposed stone country.

The Victorians gave us many of the images we hold of important moments in our lives which are taken as long established, even ancient, fact. The way we celebrate Christmas for instance, even the Christmas tree is a German tradition imported and made popular by Prince Albert. The way we get married – the white wedding dress; the way we are buried – the use of a hearse to carry the coffin, the cortège and attending ceremonial procession; all these major events in our lives (and deaths) that are considered by most as timeless have come to us within the last three generations. My great grandfather would have witnessed their introduction into society and their consequent adoption as the norm. As with these "ancient" traditions, so it is with exposed stone. Victorian society invented these things and it invented "olde-worlde exposed-stone Britain". It gave us the entirely false but strongly held images of exposed stone churches and castles both of which, if built before Victorian censorship, would have had lime coverings as a matter of course. White churches dotted the land. Place names such as Whitchurch, Whitechurch, Whitechapel, Whitekirk are strewn throughout Britain. Castles were built to dominate and to stand out clearly in the landscape, and many were lime covered to that end. They were definitely not built to blend with their surroundings.

If you do not already know this, of course, you are among that vast majority of people who accept the Victorian invention as a sort of fuzzy-fact, and perpetuate the entirely false image that, if a building is old and built of stone, it must be exposed stone. Perhaps having read this the much smaller minority of those that know and acknowledge the truth will have grown by one more.

Eurwyn Wiliam, in his fine book "The Welsh Cottage" (Royal Commission on the Ancient and Historical Monuments of Wales) discusses lime coverings and finds that, by the late 18th Century at the very least, limewashing was ubiquitous wherever the lime was available. It was, according to contemporary witnesses, such a widespread practice in Wales that it merited comment, H.P. Wyndham noting in 1774 that in Glamorgan "there is scarcely a cottage to be seen which is not regularly brushed over every month" (Wyndham 1781:151).

Today in Merionethshire it is difficult for those who do not know to visualise a village such as Maentwrog as anything but the dark blue-grey of the exposed slate stone it is built with but in 1837 it was seen as a "Charming village" with "trim white-washed cottages" (Turner 1840-7s).

Pembrokeshire, Monmouthshire, Carmarthenshire, Cardigan Bay, Montgomeryshire, Denbighshire and Anglesey are all cited in various written commentaries from the 1700s and 1800s describing landscapes scattered with limewashed dwellings and farm buildings and townscapes equally bright and colourful. In 1804 J. Evans writes of Fishguard, Pembrokeshire, "the town is small, consisting principally of cottages, the roofs as well as walls whitewashed: which cleanliness is contrasted by the rugged, dirty streets, with a dung-heap at almost every door". Ah, the rural idyll!

H.P. Wyndham's comment on the everyday normality of the sight of limewashed buildings in Glamorgan can be contrasted with another piece of commentary from J. Evans in 1800, who felt it necessary to mention their absence in Dinas Mawddwy in Merionethshire, noting "the houses...not being whitewashed were an aspect little inviting to the passing traveller" (J. Evans 1800-7s) and emphasising this as a rarity.

Of course limewash was often coloured. Several shades of yellows, pinks and reds were made from natural ochres and all the shades of all those colours can still be found as remnants on old rubblestone walls – if you know what you arc looking for. Iolo Morganwg in 1802 writes of the fashion for colouring cottages yellow in south west Wales, "by mixing yellow ochre with lime and therewith wash their houses, inside very often as well as outside". Exposed stone was and is dull by comparison.

The many historic commentaries on these lime coverings, so ubiquitous to most parts of Wales by the late 18th Century, are irrefutable evidence of the utterly false image clasped so closely to the bosom of "rubble-worshipers". It is also an image which contributes heavily to the deterioration and loss of our pre-1919 solid-walled structures. It has taken until the lime revival of today to begin the process of reintroducing lime coverings on rubblestone buildings, against strong sometimes surprisingly vitriolic and largely ignorant resistance. I am

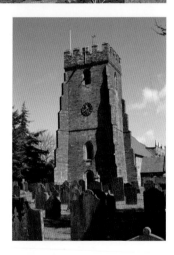

Exposed stone
(top left) Limewash traces and *(top right)* the remains of a lime render: *(above)* both found on the walls of this church.

**Victorian 'fantasy' of
a mediaeval church**
Never limewashed and so perpetuates
the 'exposed stone' myth.

sure this reintroduction will triumph over time, even in the face of so much false conviction and such permeating illusion.

The Facts

We know that if lime was available the walls of ordinary folk's homes were lime covered from at least the early 1600s and possibly much earlier. As trade and transport developed the habit became so much the norm by the late 1700s it was unusual to find cottages that were not lime coated. Iolo Morganwg's comments in 1802 speak of limewash, lime plaster and lime roughcast as everyday finishes on both small and larger houses. The Victorian rural idyll caused lime coverings to become unfashionable from about the 1880s in Wales. Over the next century rubblestone buildings progressively lost their lime coverings and with them often the efficiency of breathability. During those years the image of exposed stone became fixed in the British national psyche.

Along came cement, notably in post Second World War Britain, to "waterproof" failing exposed stone walls. With the cement came cavity wall thinking and, before we knew it, there were thousands and thousands of "damp old houses" throughout the country. Exposed stone has been a major factor in the deterioration of our historic buildings.

That needs to change. At last now we seem to be making some progress. The material correction of these buildings is just common sense, yet concerning this subject I am continually amazed at the stunning lack of that simple quality among the vast majority of architects, surveyors, engineers, builders and consequently householders – not to mention mortgage providers – and those "ripe for renovationists", the estate agents.

Through lack of knowledge this vast majority has been for years, and still is, actually damaging our historic buildings by thinking only in modern terms and relying on modern materials and methods. Unless they choose to find out the truth none of these professionals are required to have even the most basic understanding of the way solid-walled historic buildings function in order to achieve their qualifications and practice in a world which is not entirely made up of modern post-1919 structures.

I repeat yet again, that in Wales one third of our entire housing stock is of solid-walled construction.

SIX

WHAT COST CONSERVATION?

There are owners of old houses whose primary and overriding reason for deciding against the material change to their property, which would restore the function of its walls and return their home to a damp free, healthy and comfortable state, is financial.

It is assumed that because the kind of work that is usually necessary to achieve this is of a higher skill level than that required to deal with modern materials, which are almost universally designed and manufactured to minimise the effort and decision making required to achieve an acceptable level of quality, the works are liable to be expensive in the short term.

Surprisingly often it is also the case that individuals who assume this will loudly discourage others when they hear that they have decided to take the lime route, rather than what is perceived to be the cheaper option – replacing the cement or adding more "waterproofing" materials to those already damaging their home.

"Waste of time," they cry, "we've just sealed our house with (whatever waterproofer they've been persuaded to use) and that'll do the job." This is often said with such vehemence that rather than carrying conviction it loudly displays their own doubts.

Of course I've had many opportunities to confront those seemingly entrenched opinions and it takes only a few minutes to establish the fact that we have the old enemy here. Resistance to a logic which takes very little cerebral activity to understand, but resist and deny they must, because otherwise they have to admit their decision was wrong. Indeed that decision was probably based on advice from their builder who must, therefore, also be wrong but who has advised them to take the "cheaper option" because those are the materials he understands and the use of that "lime stuff" is beyond his current knowledge. If that builder wants the job he must rubbish the scary alternative.

The stimulation that sparks the defensive bristling becomes clear if the bristler will engage in dialogue. He does not like to hear the undeniable logic of the facts of life of an old solid-walled building, but finds an effective argument beyond his powers so resorts to further bluster and marches off. Often throwing a parting shot over his shoulder intended as the coup de grâce which highlights the real motive for both his decision and his discontentment "and anyway, it's far too expensive".

Of course not everybody who makes this assumption turns into Mr Angry. When confronted with the lesser known truth about solid wall behaviour (that

The long term costs
Every 7 to 10 years, the cycle of cement application is repeated.

initial moment of revelation that I wrote of in Chapter One) it is those who have the self confidence to question the veracity and extent of cement-age cavity-walled thinking who will accept that the primary cause of discomfort in their homes is material ignorance and will strive, if economically possible, to put that right.

When a contractor experienced in such conservation work prices a job, the initial response may well be the impression that this is expensive work. However, doing the right thing with the right materials at the right time can be, and is usually, the more economical option.

It is our experience at The Lime Company of West Wales (TLC) that if a solid wall structure is repaired with vapour impermeable materials, cement renders, pointing, pebbledash, etc. then those repairs are likely to be repeated every seven to ten years. After an initial honeymoon period when fresh cement works are applied to the building, the problems associated with damp penetration and retention return and make themselves evident within that time period. If the building is in an exposed location the period can be considerably less.

The moisture that becomes trapped in the walls decays lintels, window and door frames, joist ends and skirting boards, some or all of which will need replacement or repair. Moisture damage to the interior decor, caused by both water retention in the walls and the consequent condensation forming because of the low temperatures that come with water in the walls, is another repetitive problem.

If the same house was properly repaired with the right choice of lime mortars, renders, roughcast and limewash the job would need to be done only once and then maintained with those same materials, just as you should maintain a new house with modern materials.

Limeworks on an old house last every bit as long, and often much longer, as modern materials on a modern one if they are applied properly by an experienced contractor and the limewash finish can last for well over a decade before needing another coat.

The point is, of course, that repetitive works with the wrong materials and set of skills means repetitive costs and although the initial cost of the "right stuff" may be more than sticking up a cement render, in the not so very long run,

If the money can be found
No other investment in an historic
home can give so much in return.

it will prove to be a one-off that is considerably more economical than doing it all over again and again with cement, and the savings on fuel costs, once the house is functioning correctly, can be significant.

The simple truth is that using traditional materials on a traditional house will restore the walls' traditional function and will cure the problems associated with damp and decay caused in the first place by the mistaken use of modern vapour impermeable "waterproofing", whereas the replacement of those modern materials with the same thing might hide them for a time while that decay continues unabated.

Of course, there is the other result of doing the right thing. The house thus treated will last into the future and be a recognisable legacy. Generations to come will appreciate and admire it. That will not happen to a house suffering from accelerated decay, damp, unhealthy interior conditions and over costly fuel bills.

There is another approach if the mind is willing but the pocket is not. The same results can be achieved by dealing with the problem piecemeal. We have found that to return the correct function to the "weather-wall" can make a huge difference to the whole house.

It is always the elevation that faces the prevailing weather that suffers the most water ingress and consequent damage and decay. If that wall has its absorption and evaporative ability returned to it by the application of the most efficient of the lime finishes, a lime roughcast, it is remarkable how that will help the lateral walls adjoining that elevation to diminish their water content, through the evaporative services of the lime covering on the weather face. This often provides such noticeable relief that we have had clients who felt that nothing more is necessary to return their homes to a healthy, comfortable state and this has proven to be the case in the right circumstances. Others will continue to return their house to a functioning historic structure, wall by wall, as and when they can afford it, staggering cost over a number of years.

As a company, it is our policy to encourage participation by any client who is willing and able and this often means impromptu training on site, while works take place. The client in many cases is able to take over the final act of limewashing their property. A series of coats that cannot, because of the particular properties of limewash, be rushed through in less than one coat a day, and therefore can represent a marked saving in labour cost and prepare that client for the future maintenance of his home at the same time. Another potential relief for his pocket in the years to come.

To see as unaffordable the work necessary to return the function of the walls to their intended efficiency and thus the building to a truly sustainable state would of course depend on one's perspective. If there simply is no money, then there is no money, but there is no other investment in an historic home that gives so much in return if that money can be found.

SEVEN

COMFORT AND HARMONY

The appreciation of the aesthetic achieved by following tradition in material use on and in an old building can, I am strongly aware, be perceived as a matter of taste and is therefore a subject which is usually approached warily as there are not many who will admit to having bad taste or no taste at all.

This is most obviously evident when taste is connected to a person's home. Call into question someone's taste in furniture and decoration and it seems to strike at the very core of their being. Although it is nonsense to perceive such criticism as a diminishment of character, it is often taken to heart as the blackest of insults and it has become bad taste to discuss taste in the first place.

Why should this be? If, as many would claim, "everyone's taste is relevant". If we can all look another in the eye and say "it's to my taste, and that's that!" in complete confidence and comfort in our choice, then why the amplified sensitivity to the subject?

The unspoken truth is that the issue is steeped in memories of a class system that supposedly does not exist anymore and which it is politically incorrect to even acknowledge. Yet the remnants and resonance of that system, so long and so strongly part of our culture, still influence either confidence or insecurity in our personal convictions, colour our perceptions in this so called classless society and create both the resentment and the pride that is so pertinent.

It cannot be denied that for generations until well into the post Second World War decades, what was fashionable was the purview of the upper end of the "upper classes" and all that time "high" fashion was the well-spring of all that was considered good taste.

In the last thirty years, however, high fashion has become the territory of the upper end of the upper income bracket and a new kind of class system has evolved, not instead of but alongside the old one based on income rather than background. Consequently the issues of good and bad taste have become blurred by the buying power of a much broader section of society and the sheer quantity of goods available.

If one wishes to impress on others that one is part of that upper income bracket – a class in its own right – then the temptation to demonstrate by surrounding oneself with the most obviously expensive of goods can be difficult to resist. Society readily acknowledges this with colloquialisms such as bling, and bling applies as much to one's home as to personal adornment. The concept of less is more does not satisfy that kind of urge to impress.

Simplicity
Resist unnecessary flourish
in 'humble' homes.

Built to impress
Flamboyance feels entirely correct
within the more sophisticated house.

That sensitivity, which is part of a person's perception of what should go where and with what in their home, is of course, an individual matter, but I have found that those who can and do appreciate the particular beauty of lime plasters and washes on their walls and traditional floor coverings beneath their feet, very often know what looks well with that tradition in terms of furniture, dressing and ornament. To me this is less a matter of taste than a matter of the beauty of function and practicality within what should inevitably become an holistic approach to one's surroundings and the ability to recognise it.

The ability to see the beauty of simplicity and the desire to resist unnecessary flourish within houses that were obviously built as ordinary, even humble, homes will create a feeling of contentment within such surroundings, every bit as satisfying as the indulgence in more flamboyance that feels entirely correct within a more sophisticated house, one that was just as obviously built to impress.

Probably the greatest compliment that can be paid to an historic home owner, when new eyes see inside for the first time, is the query "well, what have you actually done?" – a query which does not sit well with the modern consumer-driven tendency to declare who we are through our shiny new possessions.

In a simple, historic home, and most of them were built as such, everything within and without can fit seamlessly together, creating a comfort and harmony that rarely results in any one item, or group of items, becoming an exhibit at the expense of the whole. The trick is achieving that harmony with apparent ease and perhaps that instinctive skill is good taste.

EIGHT
EXTERIORS

This section attempts to provide a coherent list of suggestions for those who would value help in preserving the aesthetic and functional qualities of vernacular buildings. This is specifically about everyday Welsh examples, but the general principles apply to the smaller historic house built of traditional materials throughout Britain.

Of course readers are free to accept or reject them as they please but my hope is that the following will have been achieved:

To have broadcast once more the fact that lime mortars, plasters and washes are fundamental to the conservation of our built heritage.

To have engaged the reader's interest in the subtle (and not so subtle) details which can make or break the final result.

To contribute towards reducing the number of houses which are being badly "restored" or converted.

To show that the choice is very often between beauty and ugliness, both of which are in the eye of the beholder, but in this case a beauty which also provides the positivity of correct function and an ugliness that often results in the negativity of accelerated decay.

Those usually vague and skeletal phrases, "in keeping" and "in character", will I hope be perceived to have some meat on their bones – some substance for consideration.

It is impossible to be entirely comprehensive within the limits of a book of this size. All the remarks in the following sections are based on practical experience and research, both achieved over a good number of years. Where generalisation has to be used on a subject that is too broad to be accommodated with precision, I rely on the reader's own ability and interest to carry out any further research into detail that pertains to his particular situation.

Llwyncadfor – surviving progress
(top) Early days; *(middle)* 1950-2010; *(bottom)* 2012: from correct function (a limed exterior), to accelerated decay (cement render), back to correct function and longevity once again (re-instated lime finish).

To avoid

(above) Cement render with 'the crack'.
(below left) Cement render (marked out
to look like 'dressed stone', plus a UPVC
window!). *(below middle)* Pebble-dash
can be visually one of the ugliest
mistakes, especially if left unpainted.
(below right) Exposed stone (and UPVC
windows and fake 'historic' door).

WALLS

Things to avoid

Vapour Impermeability: The house will malfunction.

Exposed Rubblestone: This is generally historically incorrect but is a widespread popular obsession. "Rubble worship" satisfies the urge to impress on others the status value of stone in the construction. The use of cement pointing will contribute to damage and decay of the structure and the exposed stone itself.

Masonry Paint: This is "waterproof" and vapour impermeable. It will trap moisture within the wall and once applied can be difficult to remove.

Cement Render: Often topped off with plastic based masonry paint – the most common of mistakes. Again this quest for waterproofing will result in deterioration and decay. This is the finish most employed to visually straighten-up old buildings, providing inappropriately sharp edges and a suburban rectitude that is hard on the eye and the building.

Cement Pebble-dash: The descendent of lime roughcast. Often found in areas where historic roughcast finishes were both common and relevant. Cement pebble-dash has the potential to be visually one of the ugliest mistakes especially if left unpainted. The finish itself had no specific purpose but will deteriorate the building, look awful and tear off your skin should you brush against it.

Its historic predecessor, lime roughcast or "harling" had, on the other hand, a positive functional purpose and a visual softness that if achieved correctly will enhance rather than diminish the look of the building.

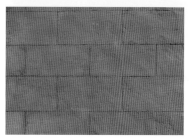

Historically and functionally correct
(left) Lime mortar pointing and limewash – the basic historic finish. *(below left)* Lime render – limewashed 'ashlar course', a conceit to cover rubblestone, imitating dressed stone and enhancing function and protection. *(below right)* Lime roughcast and limewash – the most effective for vapour permeability and thus evaporative function.

The practical consequence of modern vapour impermeable finishes is the penetration of the wall by wind driven rain, as cement based applications will crack with the natural movement of an old house and allow water penetration.

Moisture rising from direct ground contact will add to the water content which will remain in the wall causing low temperatures and decay to any part of the building vulnerable to water damage.

Currently most pre-1919 buildings have examples of the inappropriate use of these finishes and consequently suffer from accelerated decay.

Therefore, aspire to

The historically and functionally correct material that will enhance the building's looks and its preservation. Depending on the vulnerability of the building, both in terms of the rubblestone itself and the building's exposure to weather, three finishes each giving a greater degree of protection can be used.

Lime mortar pointing and several coats of limewash is the basic historic finish.

Lime render with limewash provides enhanced function and protection.

Lime roughcast finished with limewash is the most effective in terms of vapour permeability and evaporative ability and should be used in cases of exposure to harsher conditions.

Out of character

(below top) UPVC – massively polluting in its manufacture and disposal – disproportionate designs (with glazing bars stuck onto a 'hall of mirrors' reflection. *(below bottom)* A lattice of fakery. *(below right)* Altered window shapes to 'let in more light' can change the building's expression and remove historic context.

WINDOWS

The façade of a house can be thought of as its "face". The words are of course directly related. The face of a house is a visual reference to its age and its character.

The proportions and design of its windows and doors directly affect any viewer's perception of that character.

Removal of historic windows and doors, and their replacement with modern designs, has a visual impact that can be devastatingly disruptive.

Alteration of the shape and proportion of the historic window and door apertures in order to fit modern counterparts can alter the "expression" on the face of an old building to the extent of masquerade.

Lack of such visual reference removes the immediate relevance of the building from its historic context.

The UPVC Plague

A material and visual disaster that has swept the "civilised" world.

Unplasticised Polyvinyl Chloride is a massively polluting material in its manufacture and in its disposal. Basically you can't get rid of it.

Burning releases polluting and poisonous gasses. The industry claims that it can be recycled which is technically true. The cost of recycling, however, would make any product thus manufactured so expensive as to be unmarketable. At present millions and millions of tons of this material ends up in landfill.

This "economical" material when used for windows and doors whether in an old house, or a modern one is in fact one of the most uneconomical choices in terms of atmospheric and terrestrial pollution. The visual pollution it inflicts upon the historic sector is of course its most immediate offence.

Basics

In the vast majority of cases, older wooden windows that have been replaced by windows in "modern" materials and designs have been removed because of decay.

The decay in the majority of that vast majority has been caused by a combination of poor maintenance and the use of vapour impermeable materials, usually cement, trapping moisture against the frames of those windows. The wooden elements of an old house can, provided they are regularly maintained, last for hundreds of years if the walls around those elements are allowed to find their own equitable balance of moisture by the process of absorption and evaporation (UPVC has a maximum lifetime of 30-40 years as a window).

In many cases where a nice old window has survived but is suffering from the decay caused by the lack of understanding surrounding this issue, it can be saved by simple repair.

Sadly the general attitude has been, and still is, that repair is too much bother and removal and replacement with a mass produced, factory design has become the norm.

Often the perception that UPVC is absolutely acceptable is on grounds of cost alone. In the end it boils down to values. Some will think repair worthwhile – unhappily a minority. Their motivation stimulated by a sense of the correctness in their choice, or at the very least uneasiness or dissatisfaction with the inappropriate modern material and design.

It is something of a damning indictment that on Any Street, in Any Town, in Any County, UK, you can, if you are lucky, count on one hand the number of older windows in the façades of pre-1919 buildings, i.e. painted wooden sashes or casements of designs relevant to their period. The rest are overwhelmingly UPVC of disproportionate design, or worse pretending to be old-style windows with imitation plastic glazing bars stuck onto the glass or even worse still, a lattice of fakery, crudely imitating leaded panes.

The very sad thing is that all those home owners are oblivious to the weird

Bow windows
Fake 'bullseye' panes in a 'wood-look' bow window and a stock historic 'mock-up' – the 'plastic bow window'.

proportions. They simply don't care about surface mounted casements sitting proud of the frame and the very thick framing necessitated by the weaknesses of the material, which causes reduced glass areas. Designs dictated by the shortcomings of the UPVC itself which are so unsuitable to an older house that its entire visual demeanour is reduced to that of a starkly staring victim of shock. An expression not helped by the "hall of mirrors" reflections caused by the inward bowing of the panes of the double glazed units – the glass sucked out of shape by the manufacturer's attempts to create a near-vacuum between each pane.

I suppose like the friends and relations of a person who has had an unsuccessful face-lift, it's probably best to pretend you haven't noticed and ignore the altered expression. You'll get used to it in time.

There are other materials that do not suit the visual aspect of an old house, that are "out of character" and not "in keeping". Alloy framed windows, their design usually skewed towards maximum glass content, unabashedly modern in a 70s sort of way. No pretence of glazing bars here, just sheets of glass surrounded by the hard glint of pale, alloyed metal.

Wood has made a comeback but in stained and varnished shades that would never have been present on an old house historically. The darker hardwood effect, oddly coloured in a shade of maroon-brown, that strains to imitate something like mahogany. The blonde, yellowy version an overflow of the stripped-pine look that often predominates inside and is just as inappropriate outside.

There is a general supposition that these stock designs need less maintenance than a painted wooden window which of course is not true. They are painted but painted with a stain that will not peel off, and a sealant or varnish that will. The top-coat will still need maintenance but perhaps not with quite such an obvious visual reminder as peeling paint.

Out of character

Unnatural 'natural-wood' colours – too light or too dark for the complexion and alloy frames – a cold and metallic 'fishtank' look.

Historic and appropriate
(far left) Painted sash window –
'in character and in keeping'.
(left) The two colours on this
little casement are traditional.
(bottom) A new replacement
sash, appropriately painted.

The material choice is appropriate. The "historic" designs though, are obviously mass-manufactured, with thick glazing bars that throw the proportion of the whole out of true historic context, and together with their unnatural "natural-wood" colours, give the "eyes" of the house a too-much makeup look. There is further detail regarding this prickly subject in the chapter on Paint and Colour (page 70).

Inappropriate
Modern designs to replace old windows.
Stock historic mock-ups (especially bow-windows).
Picture windows.
Fake bullseye panes.
Altered window apertures.
Anything made of UPVC or alloy.
Unpainted natural-wood-look stock designs.

Appropriate
Keep existing historic aperture size unaltered.
Repair and keep existing suitable old windows wherever possible.
Preserve as much old crown glass as possible.
If replacement is unavoidable, use an historically relevant design.
Always paint, and paint in suitable colours.

Preserve

(top) Preserve as much old 'crown-glass' as possible – early glass with air bubbles and faults can be charming and is 'in keeping'. *(above)* Unusual and beautiful – craftsmanship conserved for future generations.

The double-glazing issue

If an old window can be repaired, conserved and kept in place it will not be double-glazed. Modern thinking will immediately condemn this as eco-unfriendly and that strand of thinking would see replacement with double-glazed units as the right way to go, another misguided motive for removal of historic detail.

It has to be accepted that a single pane of glass has a low insulation value, with a U-value for most plate glass of about 5.2, yet there are many options for improvement without the removal or drastic alteration of an historic window.

If we take a single glass pane as an existing baseline, below are some positive actions and their effects.

	U-value
Single pane glass as existing	5.2 (Baseline)
Fitting a standard roller blind	3.2
Closing shutters (where applicable)	2.2
Fitting heavy lined curtains	3.1
All three above	1.6
Fitting a modern honeycomb blind	2.8
Fitting **Secondary Glazing**	1.6

Source: Historic Scotland: Energy Efficiency in traditional homes

The fitting of secondary glazing is a very effective way of improving the thermal efficiency of traditional windows and retaining originality. Add to that the effect of fitting good lined curtains and the results are improved further.

There are various forms of secondary glazing, some more materially intrusive than others.

I have used a very simple form in my house. Acrylic sheets, cut to size and attached to the window frame with magnetic strips, that are painted the same colour as the interior frame and thus become virtually invisible.

Effective, economical, does not damage historic material, can be removed and replaced at will, is light in weight and easy to handle, even if you are getting on. (See Useful Contacts, page 166)

DOORS

Front doors tend to be the most noticeable entrance, and their placement means that the door plays much more than a walk-on part in establishing the historic "expression" achieved by the traditional emplacement and size of these apertures.

During the early 1970s, when poster-art was at the height of a revival, there was a poster that enjoyed great success, and was to be seen next to psychedelic images of Jimi Hendrix and block-colour prints of misty, mystic mountains. It was a series of photographs of doors.

Arranged symmetrically in several rows, as in a comic strip, they were pictures taken in Greece and the Greek Islands of traditional doors, native to those various parts, in lovely Mediterranean colours, some faded with peeling paint, others fresh and bright, some gnarled and split by sunshine, long unpainted.

There was the obvious attraction of the brightness and shadow of a warmer climate than ours, soothing to the eye and comforting during the dark and damp of our own winters, and yet there was much more.

Doors have a deep symbolism in spiritual terms in many cultures, the link so often between one world and another, one state of mind and its counterpart. To the average poster-gazer in the 60s and 70s that symbolism was more likely to be on a sub-conscious level than foremost in the mind. They were attracted to it in their thousands because the images were beautiful.

There it was, row upon row of wooden doors as popular for a while as Andy Warhol's "Campbell's Soup Can".

I wrote in my introduction of the need to analyse why we like or dislike something, so that we may learn from the experience. There is no doubt in my mind that a large part of the attraction of the images was to do with the ease of proportion, a contentment to the eye, washed in warm colours and cool shadow that made each separate image fit effortlessly into the pleasure-zone of the mind.

I have no doubt, that if one was able to return to the site of each of those doors today, most would be gone, and in their place, if indeed that place still existed and was not now a self-catering apartment, would be the jarring and busy proportion of a UPVC door, with quasi-architectural details crammed into a weirdly diminished surface area, a pastiche of amalgamated "features" that create a cartoon of the real thing. A striving for "everyman's" entrance that succeeds only in boggling the senses with its imposed pan-culturism and compressed history, a monochromatic mess of visual discomfort that crash lands in the sensory field.

And yet those mass manufactured, factory shaped and stamped incongruities are accepted everywhere, and are even chosen over other mass manufactured "historic image" wooden doors, that may be slightly, if crudely, more appropriate

Welcoming
Painted wooden doors of suitable design for the house and for the local tradition.

for a particular building. Why? Almost certainly because of cost. If it is cheaper than other designs and fills the hole in the wall, then that'll do. After all everybody else has them, so they must be alright.

So again, cost wins at the expense of the suitability of style and of beauty, for an appropriate painted wooden door, placed correctly in the face of an appropriately repaired and conserved building, can pull the whole image together and, when right, is a thing of beauty.

Sadly it seems that beauty is not something most people seek, and if they are not even aware of its existence, then it will never be sought, and placid acceptance of mass manufactured mediocrity becomes the norm – you only have to look around you to bear witness to that fact.

That mediocrity of quality and design has yet to produce a door design in UPVC that could be described by anybody as beautiful. I am (as you may have noticed) strongly prejudiced against this material and its use on and in historic buildings, and to me it reaches the peak of its offensiveness when it's used within a doorway to deface an old house.

The crassness of the stock designs are not only universally ugly in this context, they can be horrendous.

Avoid
Anything made from UPVC.
Full length glass doors.
Modern, stock doors from joinery catalogues
(except in some rare cases).
Iron studded "mediaeval miniature castle gates".
Any modern, mass-produced "historic" mock up.
Anything with "olde-worlde" detailing (oversized strap hinges).
Anything with imitation, plasticised "stained glass".

Welcome
Painted wooden doors of designs suitable to the house and its age.
Local tradition often supplies local designs.
Awareness of local designs keeps the tradition alive.

I write here specifically about the impact of front doors but back doors, though visually less immediate, have a strong effect on the historic visual aspect of the house.

They usually should be of simple design, often of tongue and groove or planked construction, some with, some without, lights and in our part of the world, used much more often than the front door. Most callers come to the back door so its design and practicality are as important in many houses as the usually more sophisticated front door.

To be avoided in wood
(clockwise from top left) Standard historic fake, with 'fanlight' in the door, not above it where it should be. Fanciful wooden historic fake from another culture (Spain perhaps?). Stock 'Continental' design with fake bullseye pane. UPVC, 6 panels stuffed into a thick-framed 'slot'. UPVC, a pastiche of 'amalgamated features', crammed into a weirdly diminished surface area. In UPVC with 'plastic obscured glass' and two 'panels' stamped into the uncomfortable proportions of the bottom section.

Welcoming

(above top) A fully enclosed, highly decorative and entirely suitable little 'glory'. *(above bottom)* A simple door-hood with turned, decorative wooden supports. *(above right)* Trellised porches can be in character and deeply attractive. *(below)* 'Beach hut' porch in a seaside town. This is the next door neighbour of the 'sentry box'.

Welcome

Slate or stone slabs for door hoods.
Slated or tiled double or single pitch roofs.
Leaded surfaces are suitable on some single pitches.

Enclosed porches built of a material suitable to the house i.e. stone, where appropriate, slate hung or weather boarded can be in keeping on the right houses.

If stone is used, especially random rubble, take care that the stone is laid properly and not on its side which looks like upright crazy-paving – follow the exposed stone rule – DON'T USE IT! Lime render, roughcast or at the very least, limewash, should be used.

Trellised porches can be in character and deeply attractive on the right house.

So, take great care with proportion; the porch should sit with visual comfort against the house and not poke the viewer in the eye.

Finally, do not add a porch at all – unless you know you can get it exactly right.

ROOFS

The roof of an old house, the material it is made of, its shape, pitch and detailing are strongly relevant to the age and character of the building.

The timber structure of an old roof is one of those delights that is well worth a grubby grovel into a roof space to see. It is among the most beautiful of collaborations between man and natural material and its visual attraction often becomes a compelling reason to expose once again.

It is understandable that householders with such delights in their attic should feel the urge to remove that attic floor and open the roof space to its peak and to everyone's view, but in so doing there is the inevitable loss of historic material, a major editing of the narrative of the building and in a modern context, the creation of a much more difficult set of circumstances for the emplacement of insulation and a much larger space to heat.

These decisions are, of course, entirely the individual's choice but in my experience the opening up of an historically enclosed roof space creates proportions that were never meant to be and can often detract from the atmosphere within the building rather than enhance it.

These are all comments about interior works that should perhaps wait until the Interiors section of this book, but while dealing with roofs it seems appropriate to look at the consequences of actions that so closely concern those timber structures that support the various forms of water-shedding material that keep us dry.

An exhibition of roof timbers within the house can become the major focus of attention, overwhelming all other detail, very often to the detriment of what should be an historic whole.

There is often another urge that concerns the roof structure, to add more space to an old house by increasing the ceiling height upstairs. This is usually achieved by flattening the pitch of the roof to raise the eaves line. When this is done to an historic building it is glaringly obvious to any discerning eye. The previous comfortable proportions are disrupted and, like a bad haircut, the change is rarely suitable nor attractive.

It is better to avoid this kind of alteration altogether but if the reasons for change are irresistible, extra light, ventilation and some space can be achieved by adding dormer windows of sympathetic proportions and design, but great care should be taken to get it right. A disproportionate dormer can look like a malignant growth.

A well designed "historic" skylight can suitably provide that ventilation and light without alteration to shape or pitch of the roofline and tends to be more in keeping if confined to the rear fall of the roof.

Straightening up dips and curves in an old roof is to be avoided unless there is a serious structural requirement. The lack of geometric precision evident in

Timber roof structures
(above top) A beautiful collaboration between man and material. *(above bottom)* Becoming the major focus of attention. *(below)* Lime plaster and wash sits well with the timber structure.

Adding a dormer
(above) An addition that works well –
proportionate and 'in character'.
(right) An historic dormer – fits
comfortably into its context. *(below)*
A disproportionate dormer can look
like a malignant growth.

many old roofs has been achieved by decades of movement within the building as it settles into a more comfortable position and is visually such a charming part of its history that censoring it can change the whole direction of the text and can make nonsense of a perfectly good story.

Roofing materials in south west Wales tend historically to be thatch – reed and straw are both relevant in different areas – and slate. Once there were quarries that produced local roofing slates that became signatures of the housing in the area. In the Preselis, for instance, there were silver grey, dark grey, dark blue and green slates all being produced within a few miles of each other, so in those cases the local slate was very local and recognisable by its colour and texture.

There are surviving roofs slated with local materials, and if you happen to have one do your utmost to conserve it for as long as you can because such survivors are now rare. As old slates wore out, new arrived with the railways and the purple-maroon of mass-produced "Caernarvon" slate began to predominate. There are still many roofs that are covered by this slate that was once said to have "roofed the world". Not quite, but it was shipped to a good many colonies and parts of the empire and certainly roofed a good proportion of the "pink" bits so evident then on the world map.

Thin cementitious "slates", produced in factories and a good deal cheaper than the real thing, began to take over from their predecessors, the asbestos "slate" in the late 1950s and early 60s.

65

Asbestos has a bad name now because, under certain conditions and especially in its "blue" form, it is carcinogenic. However, the white asbestos that was formed into roofing materials, especially slate look-a-likes, is still in place on thousands of roofs throughout the country. It is surprisingly visually inoffensive on old buildings and in some cases can be more attractive to the eye than the cement "slates". Regulations apply to the removal and disposal of asbestos. One reason that makes the asbestos version visually acceptable is its ability to weather and to take on a patina along with lichen and moss growth that can create a remarkably mellow look.

Real slate is by far the most suitable roofing material for most old houses in this part of the world but it comes now from Canada, Spain, Brazil and even China. The Welsh slate industry for reasons beyond my understanding has virtually ceased to exist and where it does the product is so expensive that only the better-off among us could possibly insist on a Welsh slate roof.

If your roof needs attention remember that most roofers would rather strip and replace it in its entirety and if you are sure that this is necessary be careful to choose a replacement material (usually slate) that is suitable.

Concrete interlocking tiles are not a good substitute. Thick, chunky in cross-section, usually the wrong colour, they change the profile of an old roof line unacceptably and their extra weight can cause problems with old roof timbers. It is very often the case that the roof covering which the builder wishes to replace can have many years of good service left and some simple repair work is all that is needed. A second, or even a third opinion may help you decide.

Chimney stacks are striking parts of a roof's profile and the deplorable fashion for removing them altogether has ruined the outline of many old houses.

Real and imitation slate
(above) Reed and straw thatch were once common in some areas. (below, clockwise from top left) Asbestos 'slates', surprisingly visually inoffensive; patina helps. The most common in usage, thin cementitious imitation slates (and plastic dormer!). Purple/maroon Caernarvon 'mass-produced' real slate; two examples of cementitious, interlocking and heavy enough to cause 'sag' in the roofline. Local silver-grey slate: small and proportionately thicker in profile, a signature of an area.

Chimney stacks - traditionally built with style, great care and much variety

(clockwise from above left) This nice old house has been generally abused and needs TLC – its whole profile is disrupted by chimney stack removal (fake shutters that would not even cover the windows do not help). A 'great chimney' for a 'simne fawr' fire, as big as some kitchen table tops! Victorian railway architecture: chimney stacks are of major visual importance – careful banded brick construction showing how considered their design is. A stack, rebuilt with its own recycled bricks; an old stack, with a more recent extension to improve 'draw' – proportionately, surprisingly attractive.

Spawned by the central heating era, confidence that open fires or stoves would for evermore be irrelevant and perceiving chimneys only as trouble-spots needing care and maintenance, choosing to remove them has proved not only short-sighted but shows a stunning disregard for one's surroundings, a lack of awareness that is reflected in so many decisions made regarding old houses.

Personally I cannot understand how the sheared look of an old roofline without its chimneys can be gazed upon with any satisfaction.

Chimney stacks and pots are almost infinite in their variety around Britain and until the modern era – when lack of thought has often turned them into spar-dashed, rectangular pimples, capped with a concrete paving slab, considering them an inconvenient afterthought rather than a vitally important part of the home's economy and structure – they were built with style. Great care was paid to detail and there was a strong consciousness of their importance, both visually and functionally.

EXTENSIONS

A notoriously difficult task to carry out successfully, the design of an extension to an old building, is another make or break area in visual appropriateness.

There are difficulties from the start. The main body of the house is most likely to be solid-walled, with little or nothing in the way of foundations. The new extension will (at present) have to comply with building regulations written for cavity wall structures and therefore will be required to have deep foundations beneath that cavity wall.

The potential for movement differential is very high, the old house moving with the ground beneath but the cavity and it foundations rigidly held in place. The result is the cracking that is so often seen at the joint of the two buildings and, of course, its consequent vulnerability to water ingress.

There are mechanical systems on the market that act like sliding shelf brackets, designed to accommodate movement by creating a little tolerance, when they are attached to the modern blockwork and inserted into the old wall. However the tolerance is minimal and emplacement is difficult because rubblestone is not laid in neat, coursed rows which is essentially what these systems are designed for. They rarely turn out to be worth the effort and expense and the only way to find out if one is going to be successful is to install it and then wait and see.

If, on the other hand, the regulators could see the obvious advantages of building a like for like structure as an extension – solid, rubblestone walls, built with flexible lime mortar and with minimal foundations – the two buildings would stay joined-at-the-hip without the unsightly and problematic cracking and both would function in the same fashion.

However, as official understanding of the basics of historic walls has only very recently begun to be absorbed and acknowledged, that sort of common sense has yet to surface.

The careful use of lime mortar at the joint of the buildings can help minimise the problem but it is likely to be an ongoing maintenance issue.

Extensions built of "eco" materials are making an appearance. Straw-bale is proving successful in many cases and if your local Building Regulations officers are verging on enlightenment with straw, the anomaly of flexibility and rigidity rubbing shoulders can be overcome as long as the material can be squeezed into enough boxes for ticking.

Design of modern additions to old buildings is the other major area of difficulty. How often I have admired the front of a traditionally built old house, only to step around to the rear of the building to be confronted by a hotchpotch of hideous replacement windows, strangely projecting additions and ugly finishes, achieving extra space by completely overriding any consideration of aesthetics.

Movement differential
A modern extension 'slotted' around the gable end of an old building. The crack corresponds exactly to the 'butting up' of the two buildings.

Visual disruptions
(above left) Flat roofed 'block' to the rear of an old house. *(above middle)* Disproportionate scale, dominating by its newness and size. *(above right)* Lifting the roofline – too shallow, and a 'kicked up the backside' profile is the result.

Working well
(below left) An historic addition on the left and a new gable end extension that looks as if it's always been there on the right. *(below right)* Rare success: a host of additions and extensions at the rear of this house, that all work well – differing roof levels add to the overall ambience – in keeping and in character.

In my opinion, as a rule, the following should be eliminated from any aspirations to extend an old house if that extension is to be "in character" and "in keeping".

Flat-roofed extensions – they will always look modern.

Disproportionate scale – it can spoil the character of the original building, dominating by its newness and size.

Hard, sharp and straight modern wall finishes – can create an inappropriate comparison by their lack of empathy. Matching the materials that the main house is built with will never go far wrong.

Modern designs for doors and windows – just because it is a new piece of building can create an uncomfortable, prosthetic effect.

Lifting the roofline at the rear of the building – often to an angle that is unsuitable and unsightly. It may be marginally better than the flat roof but getting the angle of fall right is essential to avoid compromising the overall look. Too shallow (which is the usual result) and the house will look drawn-up and hunched as if being kicked up the backside.

To be in keeping – the general principle when adding an extension should be harmony. It should look as if it has always been there. It may be argued that some extensions in modern designs and materials are successful but it requires a rare talent to truly carry it off and examples are so few that, within the context of this book, it is safer to discount them.

PAINT AND COLOUR

I have mourned the appearance of the fashion for "natural" wood finishes on windows and doors of old buildings and while there is merit in using timber rather than that clutch of visually disruptive materials, especially UPVC, the motive for using this "stripped, stained and varnished" look is the same motive that has created the overwhelming popularity of those manmade materials. Easy care, coupled with cost. The illusion that maintenance is unnecessary seems to ring the bell.

The first of those "low maintenance" windows was the Crittal, a landmark design that used standard sized metal framed casements, which looked very well on buildings of the same era (predominantly the 1930s) but soon came to be used in older buildings in the knowledge that they would not rot and would not need regular maintenance and painting to prevent that rot.

That of course was true but if left unpainted for long, the scabbed, peeling surface that resulted showed patches of metal beneath and could look even more unsightly than a time-worn and neglected wooden window. As their stock sizes were also the cause of much aperture alteration and the consequent visual disruption of the older house, their use was the first in a line of "efficiency over aesthetic" windows, none of which actually delivered enough efficiency to merit their wholesale presence.

The aluminium framed designs came next. Generally no colour but aluminium, they present to the world a "fish tank" look with large sheets of glass in thin, shiny framing. This might suit the standard housing estate architecture of the 60s and 70s but when stuck into the façade of a pre-1919 solid-walled home it results in a starkness that would probably be easier and more interesting to look at if there were actually fish swimming around on the other side of those glass sheets.

Then came the ultimate horror, the UPVC epidemic. A kind of architectural blasphemy that, unlike the other two "easy care" options, cannot be said to comfortably suit any period of architectural history – not even its own.

Both the Crittal window and the aluminium frame delivered large areas of glass that increased natural light within the room but looked flat, boring, ugly and out of character in an old house. UPVC frames, on the other hand, decrease the glass area of the window because of the shortcomings of the material. It is flexible and will not bear the weight of the glass unless it is disproportionately thick or reinforced with metal. The cheaper options (always the most popular) have chunky, wide frames that take up a much larger percentage of the total window area than the other materials and therefore inhibit the amount of natural light within the home. UPVC double-glazed windows have many other shortcomings, not least the truly appalling designs that are not only out of character in an old house but cannot, with UPVC doors, ever be described as

The Critall metal window
(top) The first of the 'low maintenance' windows. *(bottom)* A Crittall in disrepair – scabbed, peeling, rusting.

Suitable
(right) A traditionally painted casement in limewashed wall and *(far right)* a traditionally painted sash window.

An old wooden window
Still looks better in disrepair than does the unpainted Crittall.

beautiful or even attractive – even to those who advocate their use – and as for low maintenance, the host of problems they come with, in my view, completely outstrips an annual paint job (see Precious Inheritance: Chapter 8 Windows and Doors).

A painted wooden sash or casement of the right period or design for the house that it adorns, on the other hand, is not only a thoroughly practical item, it can transcend attractiveness by being thoroughly "in character" and "in keeping" with a traditionally built pre-1919 house and could not be more suitable to the majority of historic homes.

There are striking examples of local traditions in paint application, rare but still evident in some places if you know what to look for and none more attractive than the tradition in south west Wales of using two colours on a window: the frame in one and the "moving-parts" in another. The contrast against the background of a suitably limewashed exterior finish can be a delight, especially if the colours are well chosen.

For walls, limewash can be mixed in many colours but my favourite option has always been to try and match a remnant found on the wall of the house. It is surprising how often historic limewash survives in awkward to get at spots – behind rainwater downpipes or tucked up under the eaves – places the "scrapers" have missed. Sometimes it is quite obviously sitting on a piece of stone in the wall for all to see, yet it is very often not recognised for what it is.

Most people have little idea of what they are looking at and dismiss those strange white or coloured patches as part of the patina of the stone or left over modern paint. That is if they even go so far as to think about it.

If there are no remnants, then a little research into local tradition will soon give a good idea of the colours most used in a given area and historically relevant colours always look right on an old building.

The colour and texture of an historically relevant limewash on lime-pointed rubblestone, lime render or lime roughcast with painted windows and doors will combine to create a harmonious whole.

Limewash changes its depth of colour as it reacts to moisture content. It will be much darker when it is wet and will dry out to a lighter shade, so although the colour is consistent it becomes darker or lighter depending on weather.

Plastic gutters and downpipes can be replaced by expensive cast iron or aluminium historic reproductions but the basic half-round gutter and its round pipes suit most pre-1919 buildings well enough visually (there will obviously be some cases where this does not apply) and painting those "rainwater-goods" can help minimise their impact further (see Ironwork and Ornamentation). Because of the fluctuations in the colour depth of the limewash, choosing a depth somewhere between the deepest and most light of those changes and using the same limewash pigment in a white paint to achieve that happy medium on the gutters and downpipes, does a surprisingly good job of camouflage. Painting the fascia board the same background colour also helps. You know they're there but they blend so well that they virtually disappear.

Yes, a properly limewashed and painted building means that maintenance will be required but no building is maintenance free. There is no lazy man's way to conserving an old building and quick-fix solutions are no substitute for regular maintenance. If you've gone as far as this to get your old house looking and working well, then to maintain that achievement as well as you can rarely seems too much of a hardship.

Don't Use

Modern masonry paints on exterior walls.

Stained and varnished woodwork.

Highly reflective finishes – avoid gloss, exterior eggshell is more suitable visually.

N.B. see note on Breathable Mineral Paints opposite.

Do Use

Limewash, white or coloured.

An eggshell or other low reflection finish on woodwork.

Local tradition in application of colour.

Limewash

(top) Old limewash remnants, rarely recognised for what they are, although very often present on old walls.
(middle) It is much darker when wet and dries back to its lighter shade.
(bottom) Painting gutters and downpipes to blend, does a good job of camouflage.

Underperformance of a 'breathable' mineral paint

(top right) On a rubblestone chapel. *(above and below)* Three years after application to a rubblestone church tower. In both cases 'breathable' paint was thought to be the option that would require less skill to apply and less ongoing maintenance than limewash, and therefore be the 'best value' for money – not so.

Breathable Mineral Paints

There are a growing number of these exterior finish paints on the market being promoted as viable alternatives to limewash. They exist because of the general perception that limewash is a difficult material to handle and is not particularly long lasting. They are the quick-fix alternative, supposedly easy to understand and already within the average house-painter's comfort zone. Apply just like ordinary paint.

They have their place but that place, in my experience, is not on solid rubblestone walls that are bedded in earth mortars, especially if that rubblestone itself is porous and if it is in west Wales.

I have seen them work adequately in sheltered environments, particularly urban surroundings, but have also seen them fail in exposed areas and even in areas that here in Wales we would not consider so exposed.

I have been told angrily (and publicly) at a conference by a representative of the mineral paint interest that I should be "careful what I say" and answer that I can only truthfully recount what I have witnessed. The same representative declared that if used properly these paints are as breathable as limewash. I've no doubt that in laboratory conditions their "breathability" can be equated to that of limewash.

However, out in the sideways rain of Atlantic Seaboard Wales I have seen them overwhelmed by conditions that properly applied limewash copes with perfectly well, and so in all conscience I cannot recommend them across the board.

I can in all conscience say, however, that well applied limewash can last, even in exposed conditions, for a decade or more.

IRONWORK AND ORNAMENTATION

Adding bits and pieces of ornamentation that are often afterthoughts can mar the effect of what has already been achieved. Think hard before you choose how the name of your home should be displayed for instance, or what style of street number, exterior lighting, front door furniture, fencing and gates sit best with the conserved façade of the house.

To Avoid

Fake ornamental strap hinges on exterior doors.

Fake "mediaeval" iron studs on doors.

Bad imitations of old iron or brass door knockers, knobs and letter boxes.

Chrome, imitation gilt or plastic house numbers.

Modern "wrought iron" house name signs.

Rustic wooden house name signs with poker-work or plastic lettering.

Modern, mild steel, flimsy and unconvincing "wrought-iron" gates, railings, porch brackets, lanterns or plant holders.

Modern imitations of old lanterns or coach lamps especially if plastic.

Catalogue copies of Victorian street lamps in your garden or courtyard.

Artificial well heads where no well exists.

Imaginary imitation well heads above a genuine well.

Fake shutters of unsuitable design especially those which cannot in fact be closed.

Some obvious things to avoid
(left to right) 'Industrial' bulkhead light designs. Artificial or imaginary well heads. Mild steel, thin profile gates or other unconvincing imitation 'wrought iron' objects such as this 'porch'. Fake ornamental strap hinges. Fake shutters that are only ornamental – they would never cover the (very inappropriate) windows and are, again, a tradition from elsewhere. Catalogue copies of Victorian street lamps. Modern imitation of old lanterns or 'coach lamps'.

On the other hand

(clockwise, from top left) Suffolk latches; a modern reproduction door with good modern brass furniture. Good, old, iron door furniture. Simple iron 'ring-knocker'. The 'swan-neck' lamp seems to transcend historic restrictions. Very plain escutchion plates or none at all. Good, simple strap hinges (on the inside of the door). A 'proper' wrought iron gate.

On the other hand

Do hang ledge and brace doors on simple, business like strap hinges (they shouldn't be seen on the outside anyway – such hinges on an outside door, should be inside).

Use good, solid brass door furniture for later old homes (18th – 19th Century). Appropriate designs are important and the brass should not be lacquered.

Use Norfolk or Suffolk thumb latches on simple plank doors. Security demands the addition of deadlocks on such outside doors – keep the keyholes simple – very plain escutcheon plates or none at all.

If a reproduction gate in real wrought iron is out of the question, a well designed wooden gate is preferable to the thin profiles of modern, mild steel copies – they look mean and insubstantial as do wall-top railings (and other items) in the same material.

Solid iron door knockers and knobs of suitable design, finish and texture, will suit older and/or simpler houses.

Be sparing and careful with the use of electrified conversions of genuine old coach lamps for outside use. They can look bogus, as cheap imitations are so numerous and coach lamps were, after all, for coaches. Only grand houses

Appropriate
(far left) Simple, well designed wooden gate. *(left)* Good, plain, readable lettering. *(below)* Unpainted aluminium gutters and downpipes work well at the rear of this house. *(bottom)* A plain 'round' cast iron downpipe (but note the vertical crack in the inappropriate cement render).

would have had lanterns outside their doors before the coming of the National Grid.

There is one design of exterior light that seems to transcend the historic restrictions, perhaps because its form was an early design specifically for outside electric lighting and pretends to be nothing else. The "swan-neck" lamp still continues in an updated form today, that has lost its shade, which is a pity, for the earlier form with the shade is more pleasing in proportion. However even the shadeless versions outshine any coach lamp imitation, glaringly industrial bulkhead design or a prison camp array of security lights. For house names, depending on the perceived status of the house, brass plates with incised lettering, wooden rectangular plaques with the name painted in simple lettering and restrained characters, the same in simple lettering on gates or the door itself, or unlacquered brass lettering of good simple design and proportion screwed to the door or gate.

For house numbers, choose well designed brass numbers or simple painted numerals. The watchword for names and numbers is, as you may have noticed, simple. Avoid gothic and Celtic script or any other olde-worlde excesses.

Gutters and Rainwater Downpipes

Most earlier and traditional, small buildings had no guttering in the first place. Survivors seen today are of 19th or 20th Century origin. Thatched buildings need no guttering at all.

In the 19th Century cast iron gutters of "ogee" and "half-round" section were in widespread use. Today modern imitations in cast iron, aluminium or plastic are available. There is not much to choose between them in terms of profile, though "ogee" on simple houses can look busy.

In terms of cost, plastic wins by a mile and if painted appropriately (see Paint and Colour, page 70) is inoffensive. If cast iron or aluminium is preferred and affordable, then use it. Cast iron must be painted anyway and the shiny, rust-free finish of aluminium should usually be covered as well, which rather wastes the attraction of being rust-proof. The choice is, of course, yours.

Slate on edge
(above) Simply butting up to each other. *(right)* Overdone – overlapping and rounded, a tradition from elsewhere.

SLATE ON EDGE

Perhaps not strictly ornamentation, but a charmingly attractive piece of pragmatism that is undeniably decorative, is the tradition of using roofing slates set side by side on the gable end of an old house, instead of the usual wooden barge-board. This reflects the ready availability historically of slate in parts of Wales over that of timber.

When simply cut to an appropriate size and fixed butting up to one another, they are a traditional signature of locality and the urge to overdo them by shaping them into scallop-edged, rounded, overlapping scales, should be avoided. It is a tradition from elsewhere, for example I have seen it in the Pyrenees. However its introduction into our own landscape is an inaccuracy that, though pretty, is not "in keeping", because it is not "in character" and shows an indifference to local tradition at the very least. Unless of course, the aim is to present your house as a holiday snap, lifted from the photo-album of foreign experience. As with external Tyrolean or Provençal shutters, the introduction of such traditions from other cultures that have developed over centuries because of their own local conditions and materials, rarely fits comfortably into the Welsh context.

NINE
INTERIORS

"Out of character" interiors are difficult to illustrate because although they abound, to enter a house and photograph the interior furnishings, fixings and decor with the express intention of using that material as an example of "what not to do" is once again entering the danger zone of "taste" and potential mortal insult. There are not many out there who would let me past the door.

I have chosen therefore the personal health and safety route by using illustrations to indicate interior details that are "in keeping", relying on the reader's own experience to judge by contrast.

"In keeping" and "in character" apply as strongly within an old house as without but that perception is even more personal.

This section leans heavily toward the traditional as personally I find the traditional more "in keeping" within a traditional structure than a modern approach. This does not mean that modern objects cannot fit comfortably into older surroundings, indeed if one is not to live in a museum, modern objects, both decorative and functional, must be present in any old house and getting the mix right is always going to be a matter of one's own perception.

If however you have chosen the recommended SPAB route of minimal intervention, or decided to replace modern finishes with traditional, then that tradition in terms of wall finishes, floor surfaces, doors, fireplaces, stairs and ceilings, will dominate and those modern "intrusions" such as lighting, electrical wiring and switches and plumbing will take some thought and sometimes invention to blend successfully.

Kitchens and bathrooms that did not exist as such within many old homes will present choices that some will agonise over. Get enough of these things wrong and you will verge on the "modern house with old bits syndrome". If that is your intention then I very much doubt that you would have bothered to read this far.

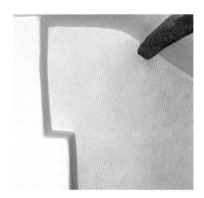

Rounded corners

Soft corners, curves and uneven surfaces in rooms that rarely have a right angle in them. Round wooden corner bead – traditional and practical.

WALLS

The Lime Company of West Wales (TLC) has worked on well over a hundred old, solid-walled houses at the time of writing and our primary intention in every case has been the reinstatement of the natural function of the walls of those buildings so that, overall, the structure of the building will be conserved as an asset to the community and as an example to future generations.

It has not been the case that every one of those buildings has been returned to the condition that compliments and enhances that natural function within. In some cases it is too expensive, and in others, too disruptive and in general terms we have found that by giving the exterior of the building the very best chance of maximising its absorption and evaporative ability, alteration of the modern interior finishes, and other already emplaced "mistakes", is often unnecessary.

Usually, depending on the degree of weather exposure, if the walls can function correctly outside there is minimal negative impact inside. Not in every case however. Sometimes a client will be determined that his old house should have the "complete treatment" inside and out whether it is entirely necessary or not. This, of course, is music to our ears and when it happens the result is always a delight to our eyes. It is in this spirit of completeness that the recommendations in this section are made.

Walls shouldn't be covered with flat, modern, cementitious plasters or plasterboard and painted with flat, modern, plastic based emulsions. Corners should not be brought to straight, rigid, sharp angles – especially around door or window reveals. The lack of texture and the infliction of parade ground uniformity is often a consequence of the perception that the house was "ripe for renovation".

Walls should have as much historic plasterwork as possible, saved and conserved. Patch repair where necessary with lime plaster, or if unavoidable, remove and replace with like for like. The texture of the plaster can vary from

Interior use

(far left) Existing plaster and limewash.
(left) 'Touchable' texture.

Internal divisions
Wooden partition wall, showing two different board sizes. A boarded partition at first floor level, sits on a lime plastered ground floor internal wall. A horizontally boarded partition wall with 'hand-sawn' differences in board width.

a visibly aggregate-rich finish in an ordinary, "rough" house to a fine polished appearance in a more sophisticated smooth house. Limewash as the final covering is usually most suitable, although a modern stable of clay paints that have a correctly matt finish and are breathable to some extent, are now being used successfully, especially on interior partition walls where breathability is not an issue.

Rounded corners and the use of wooden corner bead, where suitable, all add to the visual "softness" that is simply not present when modern materials are used. Avoid wallpaper in general but especially on the interior surfaces of exterior walls that should be able to breathe. In less sophisticated buildings do not worship the straight edge – ruled flat surfaces do not sit comfortably in rooms that rarely have a right angle in them.

Historic interior partition walls can vary in the ordinary Welsh house from the plastered stone or single brick on edge panels set in studwork to lath and plaster and, in many rural homes, wooden boarding, which sometimes shows the hand-sawn signs of differing widths of board.

Unhappily, in many smaller properties, partitions are removed to create more space and although I can and do see why given the confines of some cottages, I cannot help a feeling of regret at the inevitable loss of material and a sense of altered dimension that is often exacerbated by the removal of a stair from its original position.

It upsets the historic proportions intended by those that built it and contributes to the unease that is so often the result of removal of historic detail and dimension especially if the stair is replaced with a modern, stripped pine open tread companionway, as often seems to be the case.

CEILINGS

Old lime plaster ceilings should never be pulled down and replaced with plasterboard and emulsion paint.

Again keep as much historic plasterwork as possible. If a ceiling has cracks or sags a little, repair will usually be possible and desirable. A sag in a ceiling does not always mean it is unstable, indeed it can add to the overall ambience and is certainly less offensive to the eye in an historic context than rigid, flat plasterboard.

Again a limewash finish is most appropriate in this part of the world.

Often there is no ceiling to speak of. Simply the underside of the floorboards of the room above, laid over open joists. This, to me, is a delight, but some are troubled by the prospect of the lack of sound insulation between floors. This can be overcome by boarding the underside of the joists with appropriate timber, "butt and bead" for instance, with sound rated insulation material between. Both are easily reversible actions and can be visually historically appropriate. The "posh" room in smaller houses, the parlour, often had a "ceiling" to go with other sophistications not present in the rest of the house such as skirting boards. It was, after all, the room in which the doctor or minister might be entertained.

Visually appropriate

(clockwise, from top left) A repaired lime plaster ceiling – the 'curve' adds to the overall ambience. Very old oak joists, complete with hooks and floorboards crossing above them. A ceiling boarded over and concealing the joists – the 'posh' room, sometimes the only downstairs room with a 'ceiling'. New laths to repair an old ceiling.

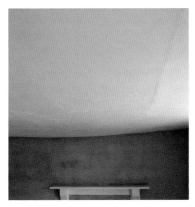

FLOORS

Traditional floor coverings replaced (often at the insistence of building regulators) with a plastic damp-proof membrane and a cement concrete floor slab, give the flat uniformity that encourages fashionable floor coverings that are visually and functionally inappropriate such as – modern, hard glazed and shiny Mediterranean (or any other) tiles. Terracotta finishes from the same holiday-inspired vision can leave a cultural clash ringing in the ears.

Historic floorboards
Munched at the edges, with 'hand-sawn' size differences.

Also out of character are:

Composite wood-look flooring.

Vinyl floor coverings of any kind (except perhaps in a bathroom).

Wall to wall carpeting on the ground floor – especially highly patterned (see Bits and Pieces, page 102).

Surviving floorboards from the pre-industrial era, even if munched at the edges by wood boring insect, should if possible be repaired and retained.

Different widths of hand-sawn boards in the same floor are a wonderful reminder of saw pit produced "boards to order" to fit a particular room.

Painted floorboards
Sometimes historically correct and attractive.

Do not strip, stain or varnish. Surviving historic floorboards can be revived by judicial scrubbing with washing soda to remove surface dirt build up (more than once may be necessary). Leave to dry and take pleasure in their natural patina. Wax polish is a suitable protective measure that does not nullify patina with an undue hard reflection. Do not seal with anything reflective.

Always ensure adequate ventilation beneath wooden flooring at ground floor level.

Appropriate historic floor coverings in our part of the world include slate slabs or old "biscuit fired" large quarry tiles – the ones without a glazed surface usually about nine inches by nine inches in old measurement.

If your floor is already a cold, dysfunctional concrete floor slab and the arguments with building regulators about reinstating a breathable floor are too much to cope with then the "effect" can be achieved by using historically correct surfaces laid in lime mortar onto the cement concrete. Do not lay good, old slabs or quarry tiles in cement or with modern adhesives. They will be damaged when lifted if ever recycling or replacement becomes desirable.

Do not seal these surfaces with anything shiny. The reflection ruins their intrinsic attractiveness and if you are lucky enough to have a "working" old floor, the sealant will inhibit evaporation. Look to see how old surfaces were laid in local tradition. Laying everything in straight, symmetrical rows can

Breathable floors

(above left) Slate slabs, laid straight onto the earth, are stunningly attractive, surrounded by limewashed walls – everything 'breathes'. *(above middle)* Old 9"×9" quarry tiles, often more than 2" in depth, laid in a lime mortar screed are in keeping, in character, deeply attractive and 'breathable'. *(above right)* Quarry tiles laid in 'brick-bond' pattern, rather than the usual straight rows – local tradition should dictate.

have a diminishing effect and the pattern created by "brick-bond" placement is most suitable and attractive.

The concrete, waterproof floor slab is a striking example of the official misunderstanding of the functional requirements of the floor in an historic, solid-walled house.

The floor is part of the breathability of the structure. Traditional floors are designed to allow excess moisture in the ground below to leave through a vapour permeable floor surface. The evaporative function that is so vital throughout these buildings, is a function that "mainstream construction" is, generally, not even aware of.

The imposition of the modern "waterproofing" concept on the floors of these structures actually causes moisture entrapment within the walls surrounding the new floor. The moisture that would normally evaporate through the traditional floor surface is trapped by the damp-proof membrane and the cement concrete and forced to migrate to the edges of the floor slab. It is thus absorbed into the rubblestone and earth mortar construction of the old walls, where it is trapped behind the modern cementitious plasters. This adds to the damp problems already created by the use of vapour impermeable materials on old houses that are "ripe for renovation".

A cement concrete slab can also decrease the temperature in a room by several degrees. A surviving historic floor often laid straight onto the earth is, in my experience, warmer to the touch than its modern equivalent. Reinstating a breathable "limecrete" floor slab is an act of conservation and can and should be done wherever possible. Building regulators are beginning to grasp that fact at last but many still find the concept too scary.

Keep old doors
(far left) A six panel 'Georgian' door, across the landing from a ledged and braced door with Suffolk latch. *(left)* Four panel 'Victorian' door.

DOORS

Avoid anything from most modern joinery stock catalogues, especially those shiny "coated" approximations of four or six panel doors. Some framed and boarded doors can be acceptable.

Steer clear of flat, egg box, hardboard "flimsies", interior fake stable doors, doors with modern obscured glass panes, or with factory made modern fake stained glass decoration, stripped, unpainted doors, panelled or otherwise.

Distinctly modern designs of door furniture look and feel wrong, as do imitation thinly coated "brass" fittings.

If you have genuine old brass door furniture in your house try not to apply lacquer – it may mean less brass cleaning but it alters the surface reflection and patina making old imitate new.

Don't use fake Tudor-esque "wrought-iron" fittings inspired by film sets or any other reproduction door furniture on doors of the wrong style or period.

Pretty china fingerplates in anything earlier than a 19th Century context, like glass fingerplates, will look modern and are reminiscent of an hotel suite.

Aspire to
Retaining any historically correct doors that you are lucky enough to have. Repairing if necessary, rather than replacing them.
Retaining existing early hinges, locks, keys and handles. This applies to cupboard doors as well.
Recognising authenticity by research.

If replacement is unavoidable
(above left & middle) These are 'new' doors, basically historically correct and 'in keeping' – the unpainted example rises above the rule by exhibiting shear craftsmanship. *(above right)* A recycled Suffolk latch.

If replacement is unavoidable – employ a good joiner to make properly detailed doors and surrounds that are "in keeping". Once right they will survive as good examples for centuries to come.

Use the historically correct type of hinge for the period and the method of fixing to the door. Often nails were used instead of screws for instance. Again a little research goes a long, long way.

Keeping simplicity in the form of Norfolk or Suffolk latches on ledge and brace doors is advisable. Differences abound and reusing older latches can add charmingly subtle variety in the right house.

In the same vein plain ironmonger's stamped steel rim locks and latches for ordinary 19th Century buildings with unornamented knobs keep the emphasis on pragmatic simplicity. Plain wooden or simple china versions will suit cupboard doors and if relevant the very practical wooden or iron turn button can work well instead of a latch.

Pragmatic simplicity
(opposite) Plain ironmonger's stamped steel rim-lock. *(below)* Simple wooden or china knobs will suit cupboard doors; the very practical wooden turn button.

As with a great deal of the advice in this book simplicity and practicality should overrule the urge to draw attention to these items by using ornamented versions, in the mistaken belief that ornamentation was the historic norm.

LIGHTING AND WIRING

This is a subject that is more difficult to deal with than most others in this section of the book, as with walls, floors, doors, etc. there is the comfort of precedence to help steer a course. Electric lighting, its placement and the quality of the light that radiates from light bulbs (both old school and those eco-friendly design disasters) have no footprints to follow.

There is sometimes evidence of the presence of a hanging lantern, the hook perhaps surviving or the marks showing where a lantern hook once was. Overhead lights and running cable to overhead lights can create visual and practical difficulties, even if such placement should be wise – ceiling heights and their structures can severely restrict the choice in the smaller vernacular Welsh house.

Wall mounted lights or sconces are often preferable but once again choice of design is all important. The in-your-face "any old-iron" look or "aged" copper manufactured fittings, with applied "verdi-gris" are to be avoided at all costs. In simple old houses, wall lights should be unobtrusive, virtually unnoticeable until turned on – and even then, where and how the illumination falls should become the focus and not the fitting itself.

Table lamps wired to a wall switch are often a very suitable solution. An attractive lamp base and shade can contribute well to the overall look of a room. The resulting illumination is set low often making it soft and interesting and the right choice of placement for the lamp will make it perfectly practical.

If wall sconces are the preferred option use the simplest of designs and if possible paint them the same colour as the wall. Avoid shades on wall sconces as there is yet to be designed a suitable modern sconce shade that does not leave one with the feeling of "could do better". Candle bulbs at the lower end of wattage help the visual dispersal of both the illumination and the sconce itself – but avoid those plastic fake candle sleeves – the bulb shape (as long as it stays on the market) is visual suggestion enough without the extra attempt at illusion.

Blending in
(below left) Boxing across the wall, between the joists carries and disguises the lighting circuit. *(below middle)* Wooden angle bead, painted to blend, covers the cable to a pendant light on an 'open' ceiling. *(below right)* Timber, cleverly planted alongside a joist to hide cabling to this light fitting.

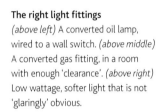

The right light fittings
(above left) A converted oil lamp, wired to a wall switch. *(above middle)* A converted gas fitting, in a room with enough 'clearance'. *(above right)* Low wattage, softer light that is not 'glaringly' obvious.

Pendant lighting, used sparingly, over a dining table for example, needs even more consideration especially with low ceilings.

If suspended from a plaster ceiling, cabling can usually be laid from above, but if old floor boards have to be lifted to achieve installation, then make sure the electrician takes great care not to damage them in the process. I have seen historic floorboards butchered by unaware electricians and plumbers.

If the ceiling consists of open boarding – the underside of the floor above – laid over joists or visible from below, then to run cabling over such a surface without it becoming an inappropriate visual intrusion takes great care and sometimes innovation to achieve successfully.

Never leave the cable and its clips visible. Do not use plastic trunking – its texture and form together combine to create an unwanted feature.

Timber corner beading – two sides of a square – tucked into the angle between the joists and boarding above and painted the same colour as the background upon which it sits, can successfully cover a cable run and become invisible enough to blend with its surroundings.

I have seen cleverly added timber planted onto or alongside joists to disguise electrical cabling but a strong sense of suitability is essential to make sure its presence does not seem outlandish.

The light fitting itself is also an area where great care in selection is essential and that sense of suitability plays an equally strong part.

If wall sconces are your choice and the walls are already plastered especially if the plaster is surviving, historic limework, then the channelling required to bury cables can be very difficult to disguise. All in all electrification with its cabling requirements needs deep thought and careful planning to carry out entirely successfully. If there are substantial areas of wall that need to be lime plastered, then that is the obvious time to run the required cable, clipped to the wall's surface and plastered over.

Switches and power points that try to look historic – those imitations of 1930s to 1950s brown plastic fitments on a wooden or brass plaque always look wrong and like glass finger plates on doors smack of the hotel suite.

Plain white plastic switches and power points, that are of our time are surprisingly inoffensive. Power points can of course be placed in concealed or unobtrusive positions and the simplest of modern switch plates is far less intrusive to the eye than a "Victorian" or "Georgian" shiny brass, over-decorated, imaginary reproduction.

Careful planning of the placement of cable runs, power points and switches, careful choice of fittings and their covers or shades and, perhaps above all, careful consideration of the quality of the light produced and where it falls, are all essential ingredients if the goal is to achieve lighting that is both harmonious and practical within its surroundings.

So – beyond consideration should be:
Plastic trunking.
Exposed cabling.
"Historic" switches and power points.
Busy wall sconces with "hats on".
Ceiling implanted down lighters.
Visible wall mounted up lighters (they look like waste paper bins or kitchen storage containers with bulbs in them).

Getting it right
(above left) A Victorian 'middle-eastern' pendant lantern – some fashions of the time created attractive 'fantasies'.
(above middle & right) Conversions from other eras can be very suitable, as can those from the early days of electrification. Note the use of 'old fashioned' plaited cable.

Careful consideration should be given to:

The form of light fitting – e.g. spot lights – be very careful if you use them. They are often best concealed and their effect when switched on should not lean towards theatrical or museum illumination. I have seen them used successfully in the kitchens of old houses, their modernity blending with that of kitchen equipment.

Placement of fittings to avoid any danger of collision – overheads too low or sconces too protruberant.

The quality of light produced – very bright, hard white light is seldom suitable.

Choice of design

There are no hard and fast rules although in general, simplicity serves well yet again.

Converted oil lamps or gas fittings can look very good in some old houses. Low wattage bulbs are essential though, if the light is not to outshine the lamp. Some designs from the earlier days of electric light, especially the 1930s, can suit an old room.

Simple brass hanging lanterns from the middle or far East seem suitable in the right space and some ships' lanterns, usually eminently spare and practical in design, can be very much at home – although scale and proportion must be of major consideration.

Simplicity

(above left) A simple brass 'eastern' lantern, hangs next to the undisguisable but essential smoke alarm. *(above middle)* The spare lines of a ship's lantern. *(above right)* Standard lamps can work in the right room.

Standard lamps can work in the right room, although again design is all important (some are horrid) and as they are more a form of furniture and can be very noticeable, placement is tricky. Shades on standard lamps are also a difficult issue – get it wrong and they can look like very large hats with no visible means of support hanging in mid air in the corner of the room.

Get it right however and they can be a definite complement. Lighting and all its paraphernalia is more a matter of opinion than of assertion, but I've yet to see an example of bright, modern design casting bright, modern illumination that works comfortably in an old, conserved property.

FIREPLACES

Perhaps of all the parts that must come together to create a singular visual concept of the interior of an old house, the fireplace is outstanding, for it not only plays a leading role in both the aesthetic and functional sense but it also plays a major part in the human concept of home. The hearth is the heart of the home.

Mankind's relationship with fire is not only ancient, playing a prominent role in our religious and superstitious concepts, but the knowledge of the skills to create it, control it and turn it to our advantage is fundamental to the development of homo-sapiens. Here was an element of life that could so horribly cause destruction and death but to learn to tame its frightening aggression and turn that energy into something life saving and life affirming was unique to the human species and still fits firmly within the human intellect.

It is something primal and everybody likes a good fire. Who among us, that has the chance, does not enjoy that relationship with flame? The careful laying, lighting and control of the living heat source that was once essential to survival?

Even though within western civilisation, we have generally become isolated from the conscious awareness of that relationship, because turning a knob or flicking a switch "magically" creates heat for one's comfort and the fire that causes it is either burning within an enclosed boiler, a box installed somewhere in the home as invisibly as possible, or even in a power station, miles away, out of sight and out of mind.

On a cold evening, give any of us the choice to sit in front of a blazing fire or a heated radiator – which would we choose?

On any modern housing estate, usually a roofscape without any chimneys, there will be a high percentage of homes whose owners will find that the lack of a fireplace as a focus within the main room, leaves them with a feeling of unease and vague dissatisfaction and that replacing that focal point with a large, flat screen television does not remove the feeling. Their answer in most cases is to install some form of pseudo fireplace, often a mass manufactured "stone" and stained wood, long and low series of stepped display surfaces with a central fake-fire that electrically produces a "flame effect". The stepped mantelpiece highlights the other culturally significant tradition that is associated with fireplaces, their role as a space to display family treasures. Already a focal point, the mantelpiece has its own place in domestic history as a setting for the family showcase.

Pictures, ornaments, mementos, cards and invitations received, items intended to please their owners and to show off to and share with guests – in fact, to declare family identity in microcosm. Few feel the need to analyse their desire to make a "fireplace" where none exists, and where, as a practical item it has no use other than as a display shelf and the fact that most of those that enter the house will accept the fake as a form of normality, with little or no thought,

The 'open fire'
With a particularly attractive slate surround and mantle.

A rare survivor
Examples of old cast iron, open grate ranges still survive, but are rarely used and tend today to be 'curios'.

emphasises the deep cultural and social significance of the heart of the home.

The history of the fireplace, the flue and the chimney is a book in itself and so a certain amount of generalisation is necessary to refine that story to a short chapter. It is helpful that this chapter concentrates mainly on the fireplaces relevant to the Welsh traditional home, although there are many instances of common usage that apply throughout Britain, especially post the industrial revolution.

The "great chimney" or simne fawr survives in many older houses in Wales, although in many more cases it has been at some stage blocked up, reduced or altogether removed. The same form of structure is known throughout England as an inglenook, a word derived from Scots Gaelic – "ingle" meaning fire and "nook" from the old Norse "noek" meaning corner or angle. The name seems to suggest corner fireplaces, but we know that fires in early hall houses were generally somewhere near the centre of the room and that smoke left through a process of diffusion, unless a "smoke hole" was present somewhere in the ridge of the roof.

A revolution in house design took place with the gradual assimilation of the chimney by society – the larger homes owned by the wealthy and powerful must have used them first – a structure designed to take the smoke out of the room at the point of its generation and which over time changed the aspect and the common layout of a home to that which we recognise today as the norm.

Many early fireplaces with chimneys were built onto the outside of the house, either the lateral or the gable end walls were used for the purpose and are known as "outshut chimneys". This additional, usually rectangular, space for the fire was I believe the derivation of the "nook" element of inglenook.

Rather than meaning "corner" in the literal sense, it is likely to have indicated the angular structure of the partially enclosed fireplace as opposed

'Outshut' chimneys
On a lateral wall and on a gable wall.

Simne fawrs (or inglenooks)
Almost a room within a room, with a lintel, an entrance and seating.

to the earlier hearth in the centre of the home that was open on all sides. A hearth with "corners".

When over time the fireplace and chimney became an integral part of the building's structure rather than an addition to it and the fireplace moved to the inside of the wall, the name remained as did the basic shape of these "fire corners". As the central fire was the heart of the home to be gathered around for warmth, conversation, entertainment, the place most suited for social interaction, so the fireplace with "corners" became almost a room within a room, with a lintel and smoke hood creating an entrance and side walls, often complete with seating, and of course places to hang and store all the paraphernalia of cooking. The inglenook or simne fawr was the kitchen and it was the warmest and most sociable place in the building.

The whole aspect of most pre-Victorian traditional buildings in Wales was affected by the structure of the simne fawr, which created an asymmetry within the façade of the building.

The space taken up by that fireplace, with its great stepped chimney meant that the placement of window apertures in the half of the building that contained the simne fawr, was closer to the centre point of the façade, and therefore farther from the "great chimney" gable end, than the window apertures on the other side of the façade from the other gable end. This asymmetry is one way of roughly gauging the age of a domestic building. If the windows on one side of the front door are further away from the gable end than those on the other side, then the presence of the simne fawr that it indicates will pre-date the house to the Victorian development, in the ordinary house, of kitchens that had their own dedicated space. A kitchen separate from the main room which therefore did not require a simne fawr with all its accoutrements, taking up a large slice of the space within that main room, and an ordinary living room fireplace would suffice. Houses built without a simne fawr usually present a façade that is symmetrical in its window placements.

Surviving simne fawrs tend now to have the great open chimney closed with some form of register plate – to leave such a large space open to the elements would result in unacceptable heat loss in modern terms and a considerable risk of the weather outside coming in down the chimney.

Lost chimneys
A lost chimney, probably indicates the removal of interior detail as well, but the asymmetry is evident in both these buildings.

There were ingenious ways of preventing too much rain coming into the fireplace. Stone or slate slabs laid on raised corner blocks, still seen on some old houses capping the chimney's flue. Decreasing the chimney's aperture by a steep and deep flaunch (the shaped mound of mortar atop a chimney stack through which today a pot would protrude) to cast off water and of course the assimilation and use of chimney pots in later years gave the opportunity of further protection, with the advent of a whole family of cowl designs, that today are the preferred options for keeping the rain out. There has always to be a good balance, however, between the restricted chimney aperture and the ability of an open fire to draw. To get it wrong can result in a room full of smoke.

In the time when the simne fawr was in use as a kitchen, the fire would, as far as possible, always be burning and the chimney itself was constantly heated. Any rain water that did not evaporate in the heated flue and reached the actual fire would have been treated as a nuisance to be worked around. Today of course the open fire will be replaced by a wood burner or perhaps a range with metal flues passing up through the register plate, a liner within the chimney itself, terminating usually in a pot with a cowl to protect from rain ingress, the rest of the great chimney's opening covered and flaunched. The use of flexible metal liners that do not impinge on the actual internal structure of the chimney is preferable to solid, sectional liners, that often require structural interference to install and which can create an inappropriate rigidity in the chimney flue of a building that, like most solid-walled homes, is prone to movement.

The choice of stove or range is obviously important both for efficient function and appearance. There is a mass of wood and multi-fuel burners on the market and the design for the fireplace and its house should be chosen with its starring role as a focus within the room firmly in mind.

Proportion is important. A stove that is too small for a simne fawr space will look inadequate and mean. To fill a smaller fireplace with a metal monster can look like serious overkill. Design is of equal concern. In the ordinary cottage or farmhouse simplicity, as is often the case with such houses, is the watchword. Busy, decorated, "gothic" doored or brightly coloured enamelled wood or multi fuel burners tend not to suit such surroundings. Although there are some eye catching designs available, in the wrong fireplace they can look clumsy and even grotesque.

The smaller fireplaces in the other rooms of the simpler house can often have surviving coal grates which should be retained if at all possible.

From the plainest of 18th Century hob grates to the almost overblown Victorian and Edwardian scene-stealers that can incorporate hooded, arched cast-iron openings, register shutters and tiled splays, the development of design is a fascinating and attractive subject and survivors from those periods should, as far as possible, remain in their given places, rather than in a recovered fireplace store.

Protection from the rain
(top, picture courtesy of Tom Lloyd)
A steep chimney flaunching.
(bottom) A slate slab covers open chimney.

Simple warmth

(above left) Today of course, the open fire will often be replaced by a wood burner – proportion and design is important. *(above middle & right)* Plain and simple Eighteenth Century coal hob-grates should be left in their place.

Guidelines for this broad subject include:

Not tearing out old Georgian to Edwardian fireplaces. One can be forgiven I think for removing those reinforced, concrete, beige and brown tiled, 1930s-50s surrounds that were used almost everywhere across the country to reduce the historic aperture of a fireplace and never sit comfortably in the older house. Who knows that they might not one day become collector's items though, as is the case with so many unwanted items from our recent past?

Not changing the scale and proportion of old fireplace openings or introducing modern grates into old fireplace openings.

Not inserting fitted electric fires or gas appliances into old fireplaces.

Not blocking up bedroom fireplaces – they form an important part of the interior architecture.

Not using modern iron fire baskets of spuriously medieval design, such as "Fleur de Lys" encrusted excesses from ready-made ironwork firms.

Not as a general rule leaving stonework or brickwork fireplace walls or chimney breasts exposed and pointed (especially with hard grey cement). If you must, don't treat with any kind of vanish or sealant. If you are worried about dirt or grit, then exposed stone is not for you – and I would rather it wasn't for anybody.

Not introducing fireplaces surrounded by "vertical crazy paving" stonework. There are many truly awful materials for surrounding a modern grate – genuine and synthetic. There is no need to employ any of them in an old house.

Not using modern reproduction 18th Century fireplaces and surrounds which are pseudo in their design or detailing or do not relate to the period of the room.

Not inserting new lintels in unsympathetic materials.

Not fitting modern copper hoods over hearths and grates they are always unconvincing, unless already an integral part of an Art Nouveau design for instance.

The don'ts outweigh the do's here, but there are a couple of things that one might find useful to consider.

Before adding a mantel shelf to a fireplace opening that lacks one, take thought of its suitability. Some types of fireplace, especially those which have a large stone lintel (unusual in south west Wales but not unknown) tend to look better without.

In the small traditional Welsh house however that word simplicity applies yet again. A plain wooden mantel shelf on shaped wooden brackets, over a parlour or bedroom fireplace is often most suitable, incorporating no further surround to the fireplace but the lime plastered walls. In west Wales I've often found traces of red limewash on the back walls of old fireplaces, suggesting the use of the colour to create a visual warmth, even when the fire is unlit. There are those who say the colour was also a defence against the ingress of bad spirits and hence bad luck, the chimney opening being an obvious entry point for harmful entities as well as weather.

Whenever this is so, I try to see that the colour is reproduced and find it most effective in creating that illusion of warmth and so very easy to understand why this tradition came about. That splash of such a warm colour in a room can be comfortable and pleasing and helps retain the rightful position of the fireplace as a focal point.

And there isn't one of us who would not appreciate a little help in averting bad luck.

A word about central heating. Real flames (using wood burning or multi fuel stoves, ranges or open fires) are the best form of heat for an old house. Burning solid fuel will draw air through the house, aiding the whole process of absorption and evaporation upon which the health of the house depends. It is an aid to breathability and the heat produced is a moist heat that does not unduly dry out old timber. Timbers in an old house are likely to have at least a 30% moisture content and this is a completely natural state of affairs. Heating by radiator which is a very dry heat will cause shrinkage and cracking to existing timbers and incidentally can seriously damage antique furniture, unless you dot your house with humidifiers to balance the moisture content.

It is better to only use central heating to create an ambient temperature within the house and to supplement it with real flame when extra warmth is required – and best not to use it all.

Under floor heating tends to be the best form of centralised warmth in an old building, as it is rarely used for the primary heat source and as recommended with radiators, calls for supplementary heat which should always be produced by real flames.

Modern magic and ancient superstition
(top) This 'manifold' for underfloor heating is installed inside an existing fitted cupboard, which will be put back around this modern, but 'suitable' form of heating to hide the visual intrusion. *(bottom)* The 'lucky' red fireplace with plain overmantle.

Below the stairs
The underside of a clever and complicated piece of work.

Individuality
Balusters not squared or straight, and a newel with an extra, unconventional prop.

STAIRS

If you have access to the underside of an old wooden stair and in most old Welsh cottages and small houses that will be the case, as the cupboard under the stairs is virtually a constant (to ignore the storage space beneath would be wasteful), then you will be able to look in detail at the construction of a clever and complicated piece of work. In simpler houses that underside will often show what appears to be a crudity in the finish of the joinery that belies the neat and satisfying aspect of the "topside" – the part we all see and use.

It is worth the effort, as nothing, apart from a set of drawings complete with instructions, will give the enquiring eye such a satisfying insight into how a staircase is put together.

Those that survive in their intended positions are not only a most important and visually attractive part of any old house but can be pivotal in the spacing and placing of all the rooms, landings and corridors within the building. The stair of a house is also another aid to dating the building, or at least the part of the building wherein the stair is built.

Fashions in stair building are not particularly numerous in the ordinary, traditional Welsh home and tend to be lumped together under the fairly ambiguous headings of Georgian and Victorian. These headings do not, however, indicate a date of build that fits neatly into the reigns of Georges One to Four, or into the dates of Victoria's long period on the throne. Fashions in architecture, both external and internal, tended to arise in the great cities, especially London (many, if not most, imported in the first place) and they often

took decades to reach west Wales in any meaningful way and stayed fashionable for decades after their heyday elsewhere.

However, the particular style of stair with its newel posts, balusters and handrails, taken with other surviving historic evidence, can be a broad indicator of which part of which century may have seen the construction of a building and will certainly indicate which fashion was prevalent at that moment.

The unsophisticated staircase within the unsophisticated house that has the simplicity of Georgian design is likely to be more crude to the eye if the house is rural. Although newels and balusters may be of the same design, finer work can predominate in the more urban building.

Variations in the quality of the work provide further depth to the human connection. To find a set of balusters that are not quite squared, or even completely straight, and a newel that has an extra, unconventional (and unfashionable) prop to help it stand firmly, brings identity to the hands that made them. An individuality less obvious in the precision of the more professional examples.

The stair in the traditional Welsh house can vary from a simple open tread, ladder-like construction leading up to a "crog loft", or sleeping area, which can be moved out of the way during the day, to the delightful Georgian style of staircase with squared, stop-chamfered newels and plain square profiled 1" x 1" balusters, or the later Victorian styles of machine turned and decorated newels with ball finials and repetitive lathe work on rounded balusters that are squared off only at their top and bottom fixing points.

Georgian and Victorian

(left) The delightful Georgian style of stair, simple and sophisticated at once – this example has a painted 'carpet'. *(middle)* Unpainted Victorian stair, with turned newel post. *(right)* 'Georgian' and 'Victorian' meet at the newel posts.

Everyday and unusual

(left) The simple decoration of 'stop-chamfering' on a squared Georgian newel. *(middle)* Boxed in stair with sisal carpet. *(right)* Offset half risers and treads on each step, to make it possible to climb a stair so steep and narrow, like a ladder (see the section on Pant yr Hwch in Chapter 11 for more context on this stair).

Stairs of the Victorian style tend to show all the busy confidence of that era and were sometimes status symbols that the owner of an earlier design of stair felt were a necessary replacement to the old fashioned simplicity of his plain, squared newels or balusters. "Keeping up with the Jones'."

In my own house this has led to a delightful anomaly. From the ground floor to the first floor landing there is a decidedly Victorian stair with all its excessive turning work. From the first floor landing onwards and generally out of sight from the ground floor, the earlier, simpler design remains.

It was seemingly felt necessary to present to visitors an aspect of "modern" thinking and design, to impress them with an up-to-date assimilation of current fashion. People then were rarely invited upstairs unless members of the family, and therefore the fact that the new thinking ended at the first landing was unlikely to be known by those outside the family group.

There is something further about this flight of stairs that adds deliciously to the strong sense of humanity present in the apparent motive for its installation. They got it wrong! The new stair has steps of normal proportions, 7" (18cm) high risers and 10" (25.5cm) deep treads but when it was fitted it was found to be an imperfect match where it met the landing. At this crucial point it fell short of the floor level, leaving a completely disproportionate 3" (7.5cm) lip – a sort of mini-step at the head of the flight. Careful attention needs to be paid to it if one is climbing the stairs in haste. Especially after an evening visit to the pub.

My feeling is that these new stairs were bought in the form of a kit, probably from a catalogue, and arrived by order at the nearest railway station. If a local

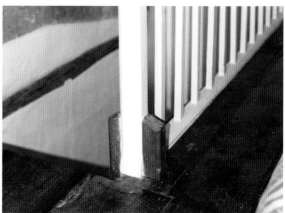

carpenter/joiner had made this stair it would almost certainly have been a perfect fit, but this evocative human error strongly illustrates our ability to bodge where there is little other choice and to make the best of an imperfect solution. Anybody who has bought goods from a catalogue knows the chances of dissatisfaction are higher than they might be with a hands-on purchase and who knows how complicated any returns policy might have been at the time?

So they made it fit.

The ground plan of the smaller, two up, two down Welsh house does not, I have to admit, lend itself to modern family living (a rather dangerous benchmark for historic homes). The usual design of two ground floor rooms separated by a partitioned passage from the front door to the foot of the stair is often, in fact usually, found to be too restrictive to accommodate the necessities of a modern life. This, of course, leads to the common practice of removing the historic partitioning and creating a single space from the two rooms and what was the passage.

This not only always destroys historic fabric and dimension but creates a walk-through rural look that leaves the stairs protruding inconveniently into this now open-plan family space. So the next act is usually to remove that physical inconvenience and re-position it often against the back wall, creating a diagonal visual inconvenience instead. Rarely aesthetically successful, especially if, as is so often the case, it is a modern, open-tread companionway, it signifies the removal and destruction of more historic material, and in this case, work of painstaking care and certainly of import and distinction to the individual history of the house.

It is always a pleasure, therefore, to walk into an old house that has somehow avoided these distressingly destructive acts of convenience, to find the proportion of the interior still intact and the stairs in their intended place and of appropriate design.

Make-do and mend
(above left) The mistake at the head of the author's stairs – an extra 3" step.
(above right) A neat, supporting repair at the base of this simple newel.
.

Of course, with sometimes tiny rooms, by modern standards, it is understandable that people will want to make alterations and it is unlikely that anything I write will change that, except among those individuals who feel as I do and they will need no persuasion. It is, however, perhaps in my power to raise an awareness among the others that what they do has more of an impact on the house than simply making more space.

If that extra space is imperative, then knowing that what you do is censorship of the past, and giving that thought its own extra space, its due consideration, could add a dimension of consequence that is so often missing in such decisions.

Try not to:

Strip out old staircases. If the space-game seems to make it imperative, think of re-using the old stairs in a new position or at least design any new stairs in the spirit of the building.

As a general rule don't use modern designs in old houses. In "rougher" cottages the simple ladder-type can be among the least offensive but can also strike a contemporary note.

Modern spiral staircases should be avoided – or copies of Victorian cast-iron ones – their prominence in most small houses tends to be at variance with any existing architectural theme.

Boxing-in parts of old staircases with modern materials, plywood for instance, will spoil their lines and startle they eye. Enclosed stairs in traditional "butt and bead", however, can be a delight.

Historic mouldings, boxing, brackets etc. should not be tampered with.

Avoid the replacement of balusters, newels, handrails etc. with others of unsuitable style or materials.

Don't paint or varnish parts of staircases that should be in natural polished wood – especially handrails.

Carpeting old staircases can be a tricky one. As a rule, don't lay carpets across the entire width of the tread. Most small houses should have no stair carpet but for those that feel it a must then plain is best once again and stair-rods can help lift a no-no into the realm of a so-so. Natural material, such as sisal, tends to be more "in keeping" in simple houses.

The do's in this case are direct spin-offs from the don'ts:

Do keep your old staircase if at all possible.

Repair carefully rather than replace.

If replacement is unavoidable then replace with a design correct for the period of the house.

Take an interest in local design and practices. Some research into materials, cross-sections and details, such as balusters and newel posts, will help in making the right choices.

Furniture plays its part
(above left & middle) Simplicity serves well. *(above right)* Upholstered items can be entirely suitable, if well chosen.

BITS AND PIECES

The achievement of an overall ambience within the historic home, a comfortable completeness that creates an apparently effortless blend of mellow age and modern convenience, is not something one finds on the other side of every old front door.

Some, admirably, will work very hard to bring their house to that state, taking time, often great effort and reaching deep into their pockets to find that level which satisfies their sense of completeness. Others seem to be able to achieve that magic blend with nothing but confidence and ease. Both, and all those in between, are likely to share a common delight in the process and, of course, the final result.

Detail, sometimes small, even nit-picking detail, can make a disproportionate difference in the rounding off, the smoothness of that elusive sense of appropriateness, the feeling that all within is within keeping. Accoutrements sitting so well that they are unlikely to be of great notice, except in their absence.

Curtain rails, shelving, handles, hooks, rugs and mats, all items that can either take the edge off that wholeness or quietly lend it a certain quality which gives wholeness its meaning.

Furniture, of course, plays its part and some will choose to make that part a major one, buying selected items to suit the house. Old furniture, especially Welsh oak furniture, will enhance most interiors, old or new, but most people will already possess furnishings that must either fit in or be disposed of, and in general soft furnishings that would never have historically been present, the

Leaning toward the conventional
(above left) 'Stripped' pine, if 'old and mellow' can fit well. *(above middle)* A Pembroke table in Pembrokeshire. *(above right)* A degree of craftsmanship reflects well, as does simple, traditional design. *(below left, picture courtesy of Mike Foxwell)* A traditional, Welsh oak 'skew' or settle and round oak table. *(below right)* Painted pine chest of drawers and unusual oak bedstead.

three-piece suite for instance, fit perfectly well in an old house if care is taken with the choice of design and upholstery, and of course, if there is the space.

Iconic modern design, such as Scandinavian style glass and steel tables, are difficult to assimilate, although I have seen some startlingly modern pieces fit comfortably into an historic interior. There is a skill though, to creating a happy blend of the very new and the old and it is a talent that is a rare pleasure to witness. It is safer by far for the rest of us to lean toward the conventional and, if possessed of the means, to furnish an old house, as far as possible, with furniture that displays a degree of craftsmanship, a quality that it will share with its surroundings.

Stripped pine in quantity should be avoided. Like exposed stone walls, it has become an entrenched image of the olde-worlde look and can be a cliché too far. In general pine was painted, it being regarded as a cheap substitute for more valued hardwoods. Once again though, if used sparingly and it is not "new and yellow" but "old and mellow", it can blend with the best.

Yes and No

Curtain rails – be careful with historic reproductions. Too many lean towards the "fortified house" look – metal rods with basket-hilt finials and quasi-mediaeval details that demand attention. Simplicity should rule once again. A plain wooden rail with wooden curtain rings is often very suitable. Old, simple brass rails, re-used in old simple surroundings will blend as you might expect and blending rather than outstanding should be the aim.

Shelving – surely shelving can go where it is convenient? Surprisingly, the wrong shelf, put up in the wrong place can have the wrong effect in a room, even before we use it to display the wrong things.

There were, in many old houses, places where shelves were often traditional. The mantleshelf is an obvious example. But a long shelf, placed high on the wall, running parallel to the open joists of such a room was often used for storage and display. In rooms with the required height, the same was often true, crossing beneath the joists, the spaces between forming natural niches that perfectly frame any objects placed there.

Shelves that hung from simple ceiling brackets, made by the local blacksmith or later, of cast-iron filigree work that could be bought from a catalogue or iron-

The right rail
(above) Simplicity with a 'twist' – a 'monkey-tail' finial on an iron rail.
(below, clockwise from top left) Traditional mantleshelf. Shelf running across the room beneath the joists, which 'frame' the contents well. Pot and plate drying rack above the range, with hanging shelf beneath.

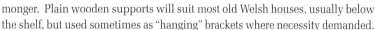

Shelves and racks

(above) Blacksmith's bracket, with a 'twist' to hang shelves from a joist. Bought in 'cast-filigree' work brackets. Traditional items, such as spoon racks with an obvious usefulness, enhance suitability *(photo courtesy of Mike Foxwell)*. *(below)* Rack for drying washing (or anything, including cats) fixed to the inside of the great lintel of the simne fawr.

monger. Plain wooden supports will suit most old Welsh houses, usually below the shelf, but used sometimes as "hanging" brackets where necessity demanded.

Modern shelving systems should be avoided, as should cheap laminated construction. Timber of the right shade and patina or painted to suit the room will fit more comfortably than relentlessly modern reflective surfaces and minimalist, shiny, metal brackets.

Often, reproducing good ideas from the past works well. Drying racks over ranges in the simne fawr are still eminently practical and their practicality enhances their suitability. Racks for drying both plates and pots and for drying washing. If there is a range that ticks over all year, then storage cupboards for those things that need to stay dry, salt and flour for instance, built into the simne far, can take the place of the old salt-box or "powder-shelf" that were once ubiquitous, and if kept simple will look well.

If the range is still used for cooking or baking, or as a back-up perhaps to a more modern cooker, then traditional kitchen items, such as wooden spoon racks and hanging pots and pans and ladles can be most suitable, as long as they are usable and used. Be careful not to turn the simne fawr into a sterile film set though. Obvious usefulness greatly enhances the effective ambience of placing such items in a suitable setting.

A simne fawr that has become simply a heat source with the fire or wood burner no longer providing a place for cooking as well, is best treated as such and not draped with items that are there just to be admired and frequently dusted and which have no current use in what was once the heart of the home. It can end up looking like the pub.

Hooks and Handles – if you have been a serial house mover, as I have, then certain things are bound to move with you each time. Over the years I have collected handles, hooks, knobs, locks and latches, some of which have been re-used over and over again, while others still await their perfect place.

Plain iron or brass handles that suit cupboard doors of equal simplicity. Suffolk latches, some handmade, others of the machine age, all the same basic, ingenious design but all differing slightly in their dimensions and shapes, giving literally a touch of individuality everywhere they are used. Each one varies to the eye and to the hand. New latches are of course perfectly adequate but because they are machine produced clones, their sameness can detract from that elusive sense of variety that must often have been the norm in a house of the pre-industrial age.

Some hooks have moved with us as well. Brass and iron again are the basic materials and although you may think a hook is a hook, the variety of shapes and sizes that form that basic "U" profile is surprising. I am a self-admitted hook-addict and will still come home with another find even though there are no more obvious places left in the home to put hooks.

Old brass, curtain tie-back hooks serve a variety of uses in our house from hanging mirrors to hanging up a kitchen hand towel and other blacksmith made iron hooks are used to hang up china jugs, for instance or, when the time is upon us, Christmas decorations.

Collection of hooks and handles
(clockwise, from top left) A singular design of 'fancy' work. Old, brass curtain 'tie-back' hooks can serve a variety of uses, such as hanging up a kitchen towel or making a set in the kitchen. A plain brass and an iron handle that suit doors of equal simplicity. Three Suffolk latches, all differing in their dimensions. Hat and coat hooks (not from B&Q). A blacksmith made iron hook.

Though some are in pairs or sets of a larger number, there are many singular designs and, whether single or in a set one thing can be said for all of them – they obviously didn't come from B&Q.

Modern, chromed or brass hooks, churned out by factories tend to look like modern, chromed, or brass hooks churned out by factories. Although it is rare for someone to actually notice that our collection is on the unusual side, especially since a hook is often partially or completely concealed by what hangs upon it, the fact that these hooks do that thing of fitting the house so well, that only a few people will be consciously aware of the design and the craftsmanship inherent in it, gives me pleasure and the satisfaction of knowing that I have got it right. They are entirely in keeping.

Again, these are such small details and many will find that sort of attention to detail much less exciting than I do and will be completely happy with a hook being a hook, whether from a high-street store or a second-hand shop. But I can guarantee that a modern, double hook of chrome or brass screwed to the back of an old door will be just that and the effort to find something more appropriate can be very rewarding.

Carpets and Rugs – if you have an old house with a functioning breathable floor then to inhibit that ability by covering it with something vapour impermeable will be a mistake. Even if your historic floor has been replaced by a lump of cement concrete on top of a plastic membrane and you still wish your house to look old and for the floor to be in character, vinyl flooring or glazed tiles from other cultures will not suffice.

Carpets and rugs
(below left) A Greek 'flotake' goat hair rug – leaving a border is advisable. *(below middle)* Colours and patterns can abound in a hand knotted Oriental rug. *(below right)* Hand made rag rug.

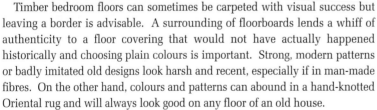

Timber bedroom floors can sometimes be carpeted with visual success but leaving a border is advisable. A surrounding of floorboards lends a whiff of authenticity to a floor covering that would not have actually happened historically and choosing plain colours is important. Strong, modern patterns or badly imitated old designs look harsh and recent, especially if in man-made fibres. On the other hand, colours and patterns can abound in a hand-knotted Oriental rug and will always look good on any floor of an old house.

Flat woven Kelims and Indian dhurries, handmade rag rugs, rope mats, rush matting, sisal matting, antique carpets of various kinds and sheepskin or other animal skins are all forms of floor covering that have no "underlay" or sealed backing and will allow a floor to breathe. Placed so that the flagstones or old quarry tiles of the floor are still highly evident, any of the above will enhance the age of the floor and will be suitably in keeping and in character without seeming contrived.

Rugs that breathe
(left) Crochet squares that allow a floor to breathe. *(top)* Antique carpets with no underlay or 'sealed' backing, placed so that the flagstones are still highly visible, will be suitably 'in keeping' and 'in character'. *(bottom)* A sheepskin sits well with this Indian dhurrie.

KITCHENS AND BATHROOMS

These two rooms, that are now necessities, are unlikely to have been there when the house was built. Historically in Wales, kitchens moved from the "great fireplace" to a dedicated room during what is described as the Victorian period, sometimes in older houses a kitchen extension was built, a "cegin fach". It was during this era that rooms specifically for cooking were included in the design of the ordinary house.

Water pumps inside the house became a convenience that most would have striven towards rather than bucketing water in from the spring, the well or a pump outside the house. This developed of course into the "tap", often with an earthenware sink beneath. The kitchen sink and the cooker are the bookends of kitchen imagery.

In many modern homes the kitchen has become a bright but boring laboratory for cooking and washing up and the householder expects to be surrounded by synthetic fixtures and finishes. It is probably, of all the rooms in a house, the one in most constant use and very often the one which receives the most visitors; friends and neighbours who drop by will often end up sitting around the kitchen table, if there is room for one.

This role of informal gathering place, which once centred around the simne fawr, has moved to the kitchen. The simne fawr was, of course, not only the main source of heat in an old house but was also the kitchen in all but name and it takes little imagination to see why the place that provided for the nutrition of the household and is still associated with comfort, warmth, shelter and even contentment, remains culturally so eminent. It is this dual role of domestic provision and social comfort that marks it out from any other place in the house

'In character'
(right) Wooden work tops, draining board and plate rack, Belfast sink, painted tongue and groove cupboard doors, 'retro' taps on extensions.
(far right) Looking through to traditional painted doors and drawers.

Material use
(far left) The use of 'meat-safe' mesh set into cupboard doors that hide machinery, aids ventilation and is 'in keeping'. *(left)* Solid fuel range and modern cooker, side by side – cast iron, stainless steel and painted 'butt and bead'. *(below)* The use of slate as a 'splash back' behind the cooker.

and in modern terms has achieved a status of high symbolism. It is noticeable that when people are asked on television quiz shows, for instance, what they would do with a financial windfall, a new kitchen comes second only to a dream holiday as the answer. Such is aspiration.

Kitchens have more than just a functional use and should have pictures on the walls, curtains at the window and objects to divert and please the eye as well as the natural clutter of a kitchen. That natural clutter itself can often do exactly that. Copper and iron pans, robust and colourful china and all the wood, steel and enamel paraphernalia for cooking and serving food, create a feeling that is specific to this room and its use. Kitchen contentment.

But how should we furnish, decorate and equip this room with its ancient purpose served nowadays by space-age technology and design? And that other upstart newcomer, the bathroom, less high profile but again fraught with the possibility of choice?

The challenges of selecting a mixture of traditional and modern that works, or choosing to go strongly down one route or the other are, I think, peculiar to these two use-specific rooms; both comparatively modern in their inclusion within the house, if not in their actual purposes. Many will say that tradition serves best in these rooms and I tend towards that opinion but I am strongly aware that tradition is largely speculative when the equipment required to allow them both to function satisfactorily is overwhelmingly likely to be extremely modern and even occasionally cutting-edge.

I find myself dumbing down high-tech design with low-tech natural materials and workmanship. The modern cooker, the refrigerator, the deep-freeze, the electric kettle, the extractor fan – while none are aesthetic boons, they are splendidly practical and I should not like to have to do without any of them. Neither would I

To paint this would be a sin!
Freestanding, carefully chosen old furniture – this general image is what the manufacturers strive to produce as the 'farmhouse kitchen'. Slate worktop, timber and the texture of lime plaster create a perfect blend.

do without a comfortable bath, perhaps a shower and modern, flushing W.C.

Entering a kitchen that is relentlessly modern, all stainless steel and toughened glass, from a room that is entirely traditional can be like entering a time warp and the same applies in reverse.

Modern, highly reflective, slick and hygienic surfaces tend, for me, to be reminiscent of the laboratory or clinic and I prefer to have something more sedate and with more warmth in its ambience. If that feeling strikes a note with you then the following comments may be of interest and use.

Kitchen surfaces should as far as possible reflect local materials. In Wales, wooden or slate worktops are eminently suitable. It is best to avoid fashionable trends (they go out of fashion at an alarming speed) or obvious expressions of status, such as granite worktops, which always seem to me to be more suited to

an undertaker's establishment, or at the very least as material more suitable for a headstone.

Machinery, such as washing machines, refrigerators and dishwashers should be kept out of sight, beneath the naturally surfaced worktop and doors to cupboards kept as simple as possible.

Tongue and groove boards can be effective as can a plain, single panelled framed door. Simple china or wooden knobs look best on such doors. Avoid ready-made kitchens that might be suitable for the housing estate up the road, however "stained" oak and beech, limed ash and all the other contrived finishes with laminate work surfaces do not sit comfortably in the kitchen of the older house. They are a quick fix solution and quite obviously so.

Using a carpenter to make simple cupboards and doors need not be any more expensive than buying a fitted kitchen and the individuality of a carpenter's work far outstrips the pretence of a "customised kitchen" that uses identical designs in different formats all over town.

There is still a burgeoning trend to have all the timber in a kitchen looking "natural". The natural look is perfect for a work surface and some kitchen furniture, but doors and drawer faces will be further enhanced by a painted finish, "stripped" wood being historically unusual while colour can add significantly to that sought after ambience.

Modern custom-designed fitted kitchens can be staggeringly expensive and often claim to represent what is euphemistically termed the "Farmhouse Kitchen". This normally means the kitchen equivalent of exposed stone. Unpainted exposed woodwork of an exaggeratedly retro look, an entirely imaginary image designed to be inflicted on a modern house, to give it "character". It is the kind of character to be avoided in old houses as much as the lower end of that fitted kitchen market – the "cheap as chipboard", blank faced laminate with recessed handles, doors hung on those sprung, surface mounted articulated hinges that never seem to close the door satisfactorily – all of which represent the kind of mass production that is the opposite to the craftsmanship that should be evident in an historic home.

If you have room, a kitchen table with a scrubbed, planked top and plain pine, sycamore or ash kitchen chairs, are all things that help to balance out the essential modernity of kitchen equipment and the painted cupboard and drawer face will enhance that balance.

The most successful kitchen furniture I have seen have been carefully chosen, free standing old pieces with nothing "fitted" about them at all, however few of us can afford to furnish our kitchens entirely with antiques.

Belfast sinks sit well in the older house and "retro" or recovered taps and a wooden draining board and plate drying rack will sit well with the sink. A stainless steel double sink and drainer with modern mixer taps and a plastic covered plate rack can strike a jarring note, unless of course you have chosen to

No chronological clash
(opposite, top) Use of painted butt and bead for bath panels and cupboards, 'retro' taps, and plain white tiles feel right for some. *(opposite, bottom)* Up to the minute shower, but with Welsh slate slabs set against a lime plastered wall to form the cabinet – the very modern meets the very traditional.

Belfast sinks sit well
Wooden draining board and plate rack, double Belfast sinks, painted doors and drawers.

ignore the past and treat the kitchen as an entirely modern area within an otherwise traditional home. That can be done and done successfully but there is an indefinable line between achieving that success and causing the whole room to reverberate with that jarring note.

Having confidence in your choice is half the battle, I'm sure, and being clear about what you are trying to achieve is an expression of such confidence, but for me the strongly lingering echoes of custom and traditional purpose still ring down through the years and inevitably influence my personal image of the kitchen in an old house.

The bathroom on the other hand is the one room where unabashed modernity can work with surprising ease and much less risk of a chronological clash. It is perhaps because the bathroom in these ordinary historic homes really does not have a precedent that goes back generally any further than the 1950s and so has always been, in contrast, a modern room.

My own tendency to the traditional still steers me in the direction of a bathroom that uses "butt and bead" timber as a bath panel and for any cupboards present and I will continue to use old or old-style taps where I can, but claw and ball footed, cast iron, free standing Victorian bath tubs are strangely out of place in these smaller homes. Is it because they depict an era during which such bath tubs were unlikely to have been present, except among the very well off? Possibly, although this is not a logical prejudice because equally, any bath tub one chooses to place in this room, a room that would not have existed as such in most traditional Welsh (or any other) homes until at least the mid-twentieth century, is unlikely to have been present before that time – however well-off one was. The grand Victorian roll top, free standing bath tub is a "House and Garden" image that has become the equivalent of the fitted "Farmhouse Kitchen" and can look equally awkward in the ordinary traditional home.

It would seem that the old bug bear taste enters the bathroom equation and that results in the equally old debates over personal preference. Irredeemably modern and up-to-the-minute designs run far less risk of seeming out of place in a bathroom than such design does in a kitchen. The bathroom does not seem to call out for the kind of balance between times that the culture of the kitchen demands, except perhaps in the choice of material. Plastic baths, shower trays and other fittings for instance – especially bath panels – never seem right to the eye in any old home.

TEN

FALLING OFF THE BANDWAGON

When I first became involved in the lime revival very few people in Wales had even heard of it as a material for use in building and certainly had no understanding of its importance as the fundamental material needed to achieve success in conserving historic structures.

Even ten years ago, most would think of lime as a kind of lemon that lends its name to a particularly lurid shade of green. Gradually there has been a penetration of public awareness started at grass roots level by local publicity – articles written in newspapers and local magazines, radio broadcasts and a gradual increase in interest by national television in "restoration" (a much abused and misused term by the media and thus the public). Where TV leads by the nose, the public face must follow and heightened interest in our built heritage led to more notice being taken of those of us that were labelled at the time as "lime loonies".

In Wales we use lime's remarkable ability to relieve damp problems in solid-walled structures as an aid to achieving public awareness. We targeted those that were still suffering in spite of all the modern preventions and cures, through local media and by speaking and demonstrating at as many events and venues as possible.

Examples of success in the alleviation of damp and the particular beauty brought to the "cured" building by the use of lime, helped to build awareness gradually to the point where now if asked, the average person in the street is likely to know at the very least, that cement is bad for old buildings and lime is good.

They might not know why this is, but those fundamental facts mean a much increased readiness to accept the material.

The sustainability issue, with its great trail of misunderstandings, poorly thought through policy, commercial hypocrisy and chances for exploitation, has brought lime's very strong green credentials into sharper focus. Those that are able to use the material successfully in its many forms are experiencing a rise in demand. This of course presents opportunities to others who see an increasing market as a bandwagon and consequently there is a growing number of people claiming to understand the use of lime as a building material.

The chances of poorly carried out lime work or even work that fails completely, are very high indeed if the practitioner is not fully aware of best practice. The consequences of that lack of understanding can be expensive, not to say disappointing.

Steps to conservation
(anti-clockwise, from top left) Scaffold up, cement off. Completely wrapped scaffold: this creates a controllable environment between the hessian and the building. Protection down after at least 14 days – limework complete and successful for the long term. This asymmetric façade indicates the presence of a simne fawr. *(courtesy of Tim and Mich Peter)*

I am becoming increasingly aware of those consequences, as a rising number of the disappointed make contact to have their lime work's failure diagnosed and corrected. One of the extremely worrying results of this exploitation is the tendency for both the exploiter and the exploited to blame the material and revert to cement and other vapour impermeable materials. After decades of struggling to highlight lime's positive properties, such setbacks caused by ignorance and cynical usage are both frustrating and a great danger to the conservation of our built heritage.

There are some basic actions that can be taken to ensure, as far as is possible, that the person who claims to understand how to use lime mortars, plasters, renders, roughcasts and washes on your solid-walled home, really does know what he's doing.

Always view examples of previous work and speak to previous clients – nothing demonstrates initial knowledge and quality of work as well as supposedly completed work.

Ask these questions of the potential contractor:
1. What kind of lime does he intend to use? Lime putty or hydraulic lime?
2. What will be the ratio of the mix?
3. What kind of aggregate will he use?
4. Does the substrate where the lime is to be emplaced, need preparation and if so why?
5. If plastering or rendering, how many coats will be put up and will he use hair in the mix? And if so what kind of hair and for which coat?
6. How will he control carbonation, for how long and why is it important?

The potential contractor should have the following answers if he is fully competent in the use of this material:

1. Either lime putty or hydraulic lime can be relevant, although the use of lime putty is more rare. If he is unaware that more than one kind exists then knowledge is minimal. At present three natural hydraulic limes are available on the market, designated NHL (Natural Hydraulic Lime) and labelled as follows – NHL 2, NHL 3.5 and NHL 5 – each of varying compressive strengths and each of varying flexibility and permeability.

   The most readily available and therefore the most likely "correct" answer will be NHL 3.5. If nothing is known about the above – beware.

2. If he intends to use lime putty, he should know that the general use ratio is three aggregate to one putty. If hydraulic lime, then the general use ratio should be two aggregate to one natural hydraulic lime.

3. The answer to this should be specific. For lime mortars, plasters and renders, only a sharp sand should be used and importantly that sharp sand should have a wide variety of particle sizes. A well graded sharp sand is essential to success.

4. All lime works should be emplaced onto a wetted substrate. A dry surface will draw the moisture out of the lime mix causing shrinkage, cracking and possible separation from that substrate.

5. Hair should be used in the base coat for two coat work and the first two coats of three coat work. The hair should be horse or goat hair (there is a synthetic variant made of a plastic material which is much less desirable).

6. This answer is important as it is often a cause of failure among the inexperienced. All exterior lime works should be protected from direct

Hessian protection
(above left) Hessian from chimney base to ground level: complete protection. *(above right)* Two weeks after completion will see adequate carbonation has taken place. NB lime will not carbonate below 5°C – however well wrapped! *(courtesy of Deian and Kelly Phillips)*

How not to protect new limework
This is a very large project and on the day that this picture was taken, a fresh drying breeze was blowing and direct, strong sunlight falling onto this wall. A single sheet of thin hessian, hanging directly against the new work is much less than adequate. The lime mortar beneath this 'protection' will dry out and carbonate far too fast for it to achieve its full potential, which means it will not last as long as it could and should. This work was being carried out by a large 'professional' company, who should know better. This is not best practice!

rainfall, direct sunshine and direct wind contact to prevent fast drying, which leads to weak carbonation, shrinkage and cracking.

The protection should consist of a completely wrapped scaffold using a medium to heavy weight hessian – plastic sheeting and similar can work but are less effective – not casually draped pieces of cloth directly over the wet work and not loosely hung material that flaps in the breeze. The lime work behind this protection should be kept moist by gentle spraying with water for a minimum of 14 days before the protection is removed.

If anyone should offer to do lime work to your house without comprehensive protection built into the price – find somebody else – unprotected lime work has a strong likelihood of weakness and early failure and the contractor has less than the required knowledge for comprehensive success.

It is a scientific fact that properly protected hydraulic lime finishes, kept damp for 14 days, can double their compressive strength during that period.

Finally, do not rely on the knowledge and therefore the specification of an architect or surveyor without question. As stressed throughout this book (and in "Precious Inheritance"), the vast majority of these professionals are unaware of the particular function of solid-walled structures and their knowledge of suitable material emplacement and its effects is often limited. If employing such professionals, make sure that they definitely declare their understanding of traditional material use in historic buildings.

ELEVEN

THE LEGACY SUSTAINED

The next few pages are dedicated to images of some "ordinary" historic buildings. In terms of numbers, examples such as these should really be termed extraordinary, as the approach they represent affects such a tiny percentage of the half million or so solid-walled, pre-1919 homes in Wales.

The owners have all absorbed with enthusiasm and relish the principles of the material conservation of their buildings. In all cases that has been their initial and driving motive. That motive has taken them beyond the correction of exterior malfunction alone and has "come inside", creating in the process delightful visual harmonies that are completely appropriate to such buildings. Not only do they look well but they adhere to the proper understanding of the potential for true sustainability within these structures. They recreate the conditions that lead to a marked improvement in fuel consumption and energy performance.

They are acts that are therefore of high value, not only to the individual home owner, but to the whole community. They will be consequential into the long term future and are all "in keeping" and "in character" of course.

These buildings have all had their balance restored to them and if maintained within the principles of that balance, they will last for centuries to come. They are successful examples of a sustainable legacy, a legacy that has been misunderstood, mistreated, under-valued and laid waste by the decay and destruction caused by official and popular ignorance for far too long.

RIVER BEND COTTAGE

HOOK, SOUTH PEMBROKESHIRE

Records of the existence of this building go back to 1777, but it is almost certainly the case that the cottage pre-dates that year. Different stages of building work and variations in the quality of the stonework, discovered during repair and conservation, suggest its existence prior to the simple rectangular shape shown on an estate map of that date. Further records show the development of River Bend Cottage, a rearwards extension in the tithe map of 1841 for instance and from the census of 1841, we know that William Evans and his wife Margaret, both in their late fifties were living there and that William was a bargeman.

The cottage is built as its present name suggests on a bend in the then navigable river Cleddau on high land overlooking the site of Hook Quay, which was the shipping point for the coal produced in the very active Hook mines.

The censuses of 1851 and 1861 show the inevitable social decline that came to most ordinary folk in those days with the advancement of age. William was a lighterman in 1851, but is described as a pauper ten years later at the age of 76 and his wife Margaret is listed as a school mistress in 1861.

There is a strong verbal tradition in the village that the cottage was at one time both a bakery, serving the colliers and a small school, serving their children. 1871 shows Margaret as a widow, still living there, but she too has gone by the census of 1881 and between then and 1901 an expansion of the Hook mines including the digging of two tunnels used to transport coal from the mines to the quay by tram, caused a population explosion in the area that renders definitive records of habitation at River Bend Cottage unreliable.

A rapid turnover of inhabitants and multiple occupation creates confusion but as the railways became more dominant in the transport of coal and the river gradually silted up, the quay became less busy and finally redundant.

Further records show steady tenancy of the cottage until 1920, when the estate that owned it sold it to a William Bowen who worked at the colliery and he, his wife Esther and their family bring in the modern age.

Their daughter known later to all in village as "Aunty Molly" was driven from the cottage by fire in 1945 and it would appear that the building remained damaged and empty for many years. We know that Aunty Molly and her husband were back in the 1970s and a flat-roofed, one storey extension, typical of that decade, housing a kitchen and a bathroom came with them.

The 'river bend'
The cottage is built on a bend in the then navigable river Cleddau on high land overlooking the site of Hook Quay.

Modern material abuse
River Bend Cottage in the 1970s. Corrugated asbestos roof, cement and masonry paint dominate. Note the flat roofed extension on the gable end.

Always damp?

(above left) The llaethdy, now a dry and useful room. *(above right)* Sandy's clever use of 'willow fencing' to re-create a missing partition.

A photograph of that time shows that modern thinking and materials now dominated this little building. Cement pebble-dash and corrugated roofing are evident and Aunty Molly was remembered to have regretted the use of cement as it "gave her damp where there had never previously been damp", an unsurprising insight to conservators of historic buildings.

The llaethdy (dairy), a room within the house as was the norm with such buildings, was said to "have always been very damp" and that use of the word "always" is indicative of the prevailing lack of understanding which resulted in these buildings being perceived as "damp old houses". The damp was induced by ignorance of the function of the solid wall and the loss of skills required to use vapour permeable lime rather than the impermeability of the cement that now prevailed. The proof that this loss of function was the cause of the llaethdy "always being very damp" is the fact that the same room with its breathability restored is now a dry and useful room as it "always" was before the cement and plastic paint age.

When Sandy John took possession of River Bend Cottage in 2008 it was an "exposed" stone, cement pointed image of the fantasy that prevailed and still does of an historic building. Inside, more exposed stone and cement render continued the received imagery and the "walk through rural" effect had been achieved by the removal of historic partition walls and the staircase, which was replaced diagonally across the rear wall of the room by a modern one. This of course is all familiar ground.

For Sandy, it was at the time a daunting prospect, as in her own words "the cottage had absolutely no heating, the walls were running with moisture and the

121

cement was damp-stained in many places, the chimneys both leaked. It had a damp, dark, slightly wild, somewhat forbidding air and I began to wonder whether it was a sensible idea at all."

Sandy sincerely wished to "do the right thing" by her gloomy little cottage and began some basic research and self education, which led her to attend a SPAB Homeowners weekend course at which the author was teaching. Although the major stimulus for attending the course was to learn what should be done to relieve the chronic dampness within River Bend Cottage, those courses taught the overriding principle of minimal intervention, to conserve rather than restore and restore only if there was irreproachable evidence of what was there to be restored.

Sandy had a particular concern. There was a brick built "thing" in the great fireplace and at the time Sandy had no idea if "the beastie" as she called it, was an historic part of the building or a modern "feature". Its shape was that of some sort of enclosed oven, yet it had no access to lay fire or to actually cook anything. Unwilling to remove something that may be of historic significance, and the story of this little building once being a bakery, suggested that a bread oven would have been in the house at some stage, "the beastie" proved to be of deep concern.

We were able to put her mind at rest, when sometime later we visited to discuss the whole matter of repair and conservation and discovered that it was, in estate agent speak, a "character feature", but not an original one.

Somebody's imagination had got the better of them and this "thing" was a cement built fantasy of a bread oven, based on an image, probably received from one of those pizza restaurants that bake their wares in front of the clientele as part of the show. Ironically, it had been built in such a position that it actually hid from sight the wide scoop in the back wall of the simne fawr that formed the niche that once really did contain the bread oven.

Sandy and her mother do not yet permanently live in River Bend Cottage although after three separate tranches of work, it is now perfectly habitable. At the time of writing, there is still some interior lime plastering to be done to bring the whole thing together but Sandy's approach has been a wonderful example of patience and determination to get it right. She decided to split the works required into separate annual visits, setting a target each year and spreading the costs over a four year period.

The re-liming, inside and out, the installation of appropriate windows, the use of differently pigmented limewash in different rooms, researched detail in the use of handles, hooks and hinges, a superb sense for the right furniture and thoughtful use of design for wood burning stoves, plus Sandy's very clever use of willow garden fencing as a room divider, have transformed what was a "damp, dark, slightly wild and forbidding" building into one that is a warm, inviting, comfortable home. It feels says Sandy, "as if it is coming to life again and now returned to the natural protection of lime is moving on into the next two hundred years of its life."

The 'Beastie'
An historic part of the building or a modern "feature"?

Outside and in
(opposite, clockwise from top left)
A suitable casement window. Interior of casement – with appropriate 'furniture'. Gable end with 'outshut' upstairs fireplace and chimney, an 'in character' casement window and slate on edge at the eaves. Traditional furniture, floor and wall finishes and real flame heating – thoughtful choice of the right wood burners for the right fireplaces.

Determination to get it right
(far left) A new but historically correct cupboard door. *(left top)* Lime plaster texture and pigmented limewash. *(left bottom)* Attention to hinges and handles. *(below)* Green pigmented limewash and the 'right' furniture in a bedroom.

River Bend Cottage has had its natural abilities reinstated. This revival allows the walls to make use of their traditional function of absorption and evaporation of moisture, naturally controlling its levels and preventing its entrapment. Standing beside a tarmac surfaced road, with camber that causes rainwater run-off towards the front of the house, the installation of a grill-covered drainage channel across the length of the façade to intercept and take away excess water, effectively reduces the amount of moisture that the front wall of River Bend Cottage has to deal with. Conservation of historic buildings in Wales is nearly always about water management.

Careful owners
Sandy John and her mother Madge.

That reinstated function allows maximum use to be made of the positive effects of the thermal mass inherent in these solid rubblestone walls – the ability of a building to absorb heat over a period of higher temperatures and release it when ambient temperatures fall – a property not considered in current energy assessment tools, which makes a nonsense of the accuracy of the current methods of calculation for one third of our housing stock in Wales.

The abilities of thermal mass and its blindingly obvious positive effects have been revived in River Bend Cottage and the consequent visual enhancement of this delightful traditional home is both a functional and aesthetic asset to those that live in it and by extension the wider community. The conservation of a little piece of local history, an act which also provides the direct effect of CO_2 reduction, is of consequence to us all.

Historical Context

The first recorded existence of River Bend Cottage was in 1777 and in that year, when a small oblong was printed onto an estate map, representing the tiny enclosure that was the cottage, other events were taking place in the world, that in their display here will give some texture and significance to that one year, over 230 years ago, during which:

Thomas Gainsborough painted "The Watering Place".

Richard Sheridan's "The School for Scandal" plays at the Theatre Royal, Drury Lane. Sheridan's rhyming commentary in praise of women, would perhaps be deemed "sexist" today – though his words transcend time and political correctness:

"Here's to the maiden of bashful fifteen,

Here's to the widow of fifty,

Here's to the flaunting, extravagant queen,

and here's to the housewife that's thrifty."

Mozart's Concerto No 9 for Pianoforte and Orchestra is played for the first time in Salzburg.

Following the Declaration of Independence on 4th July 1776 and a string of defeats for the rebellious American colonists, George Washington's Continental Army defeats the British at Princeton, overwinters at Valley Forge and despite severe conditions and losses goes on to defeat the British again at the Battle of Monmouth the following year. [The American War of Independence will continue to be fought on land and at sea until final British defeat in 1881 and the fledgling United States of America becomes a reality].

Philosopher Thomas Paine's "Common Sense" circulates in pamphlet form and is a major influence on public opinion of the revolutionary cause in the American colonies.

Rio de Janeiro becomes the capital of the Portuguese colony of Brazil, succeeding the former administrative centre of Bahia.

FELIN GANOL
(MIDDLEMILL), LLANRHYSTUD, CEREDIGION

A watermill and its house have been standing on this site since at least 1732 and almost certainly a good deal longer. Virtually surrounded now by modern housing (bungalows predominate) it sits like precious ore amidst the dross.

Once it stood at what would have been the centre of the village, at a crossroads by a ford, which was a conjunction of the main routes to Aberystwyth, Lampeter and Cardigan until the arrival of the toll road in the late eighteenth century. In a field close by where there is now a school, reputedly, once stood a twelfth century Knight's Hospitallers' Infirmary, the site mentioned in the mill records as Ysbyty Haul, or Spitty Hall.

Mediaeval institutions such as Ysbyty Haul were nearly always centres of activity and skills and by the very nature of its function this infirmary would have been a destination.

Feeding the Hospitallers, those they cared for, visitors and travellers, would of course have been a priority and given that set of circumstances, it is not hard to speculate that Felin Ganol has been the site of a mill since at least that time.

Listed by CADW as "a rare example of a west Wales corn mill, complete with machinery", that completeness has been achieved by clever, knowledgeable and skilful repairs to the working parts of the mill.

Andy and Ann Parry moved into Felin Ganol in 2006 with their family, taking over from the previous owners whose intention had been to restore the mill to a working condition and to start producing flour once again. Some good work was carried out by those owners on the cast-iron wheel, replacing the wooden elements that were beyond repair but the bearings on the great central axle had deteriorated to the point of seizure and perhaps the prospect of the logistics and effort required to replace them may have proved a daunting task too far, not to mention the repairs needed on the mill's internal working parts.

Initially, Andy tells me, the lovely old house with its outbuildings was the major attraction, as together they could provide adequate accommodation for their family, which was not an inconsiderable concern. They had seven offspring and Ann's mother to house.

Both Andy's and Ann's professional backgrounds of agricultural research, with Ann specialising in cereal pathology, provided the plinth for the gradual growth of what most would see as a towering ambition – to complete the task that the previous inhabitants had tried to do, hopefully without encountering hurdles that were beyond their powers to clear, or at the very least to clamber over.

Exterior conservation
All vapour impermeable materials were removed and replaced with lime mortar and wash – the limewash colour was one of several found as remnants on the buildings.

 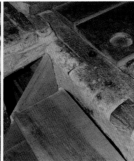 

I can tell you, as I write in 2013, that Felin Ganol milled its first "Parry flour" in 2009 and so their high ambition has been achieved by a combination of skill, knowledge (a lot acquired "on the job") and above all determination. Felin Ganol is now a working water mill producing high quality flours commercially.

I am full of admiration, not only for their tenacity, but also for the essential mixture of sensitivity and pragmatism that they have shown in the repair and conservation of those functional and sometimes beautiful working parts that now, on command, rumble into massive movement, the whole ancient structure trembling like something alive. It is a sight, a sound and smell as old as the mill itself – more, it is as ancient as the concept of water milling itself. If you have never experienced the extreme evocation of first hand witness to this historic process, a process that has been counted as a primary essential to man's survival and development, then it is something you should do. That direct connection to the past, the fact that what you see, hear, smell and touch is truly as it always was. The inclusion of these senses makes it a unique and memorable experience.

I met the Parrys at an AGM of the Welsh Mills Society, where I had been invited to speak and to give a presentation on the facts of material and historic conservation of those buildings, most, if not all, being solid, rubblestone walled structures. As an adjunct to that presentation I sold copies of Precious Inheritance to any delegates who wished to buy and among those were Andy and Ann Parry.

It was not long before they made contact and after visiting Felin Ganol a conservation plan for the exteriors of the main complex, house and mill was agreed and this, of course, included the removal of all vapour impermeable materials and their replacement with lime mortars and washes. It was while this not inconsiderable task was underway that I became aware of the extent of the works that the Parrys had already carried out to the working parts of the mill.

Those working parts have names that in themselves are archaic links in the chain of continuity – the pit-wheel on its wheel shaft that meshes with a wallower, above which a wooden spur-wheel drives two iron stone-nuts set on oak bridge-trees. There are the hurst frame, the layshaft and wooden toothed

What SPAB would call 'honest repairs' *(above & opposite)* Andy Parry and his son William used new timber to repair and replace where necessary: spur wheel, flour chutes, steps and stairs. The old timber and the new stand together.

bevel-cog. Massive timbers and rough cut joists support the grinding floor, where two enclosed grindstone wheels turn beneath horse-framed hoppers that feed then with grain.

Understanding the terminology of the construction and use of each item, is by no means essential for the enjoyment of the layman, their sounds can be enough to be part of that sense of the age of this most ancient process of milling.

Those parts that now rumble and creak into ponderous and powerful production have had repairs made to them by Andy, with the predominant help of his son William. The repairs to the timber parts, carried out in new wood that looks fresh and bright against the aged and worn older timber are what SPAB would call "honest repairs". There has been, I am glad to say, no attempt to artificially age those repairs and the effect beautifully highlights their extent and the contrast of new material, often scarfed and jointed directly into the old, draws the eye to detail. Detail that is historically correct in its shape and function, each repair completely of traditional form, which enhances the whole experience.

Repairs such as these would once have been a matter of course and maintenance and would have been spread over a good period of the mill's long

The miller mulls it over
The deeply satisfying atmosphere
of the interior.

life. The inactivity that this mill (and most others that still survive) has endured, means moving parts that have been stationary for far too long will create the conditions that require such intervention, to once again "get the wheels turning".

The mill pond, the reservoir of constantly renewable power required to drive the machinery, needed to be cleared out and its feed from the river reinstated. The race, the channel that directs water flow from the pond onto the wheel, had to be dug out and the great wheel itself needed replacement bearings. All so easy to say and to write but all so challenging, both physically and mentally, to actually carry out.

I hope some of the deeply satisfying atmosphere of the repaired and conserved interior of the mill comes across in the illustrations accompanying this text.

The exterior lime works have an important role to play functionally in the ability of these buildings to survive long into the future and they have succeeded in their aesthetic contribution. Using a limewash colour as a finish that is relevant to the buildings, one of several found to have been used on them over the centuries, adds to an undeniable feeling of visual contentment in the overall success of this family led conservation project. It is, perhaps, the cherry on the cake, the strongest compliment we could have offered to the outstanding success that the Parry family have achieved. This is a building that brings beauty of function into focus and as with virtually all pre-industrial age, "everyday" buildings, its creation was the cause of truly negligible pollution, not only in the mechanical sense but the vast majority of the materials from which it is made, stone, earth, lime and timber, would have been sourced locally – probably

Inside and out

(above left & middle) Much of the interior remains untouched; doors and their locks unchanged for decades – the marks of an earlier, larger lock and latch can be seen. *(above right & below)* Entrances to a different world. The flap for the essential 'mill cat' evident above.

Visual contentment
The working part of the mill complex.

within two square miles of where Felin Ganol stands and those materials were and are recyclable.

Its longevity confirmed and reassured into future centuries by the re-use of a material that has returned their natural function to its walls, a material that in its initial use actually absorbs carbon dioxide, Felin Ganol could continue to produce food by a mechanical means that creates nothing in the form of waste pollution and, as long as rain continues to fall in Wales, has a constantly renewable source of power. That is sustainability.

A more sustainable approach
(left) The Mill House. *(top)* The repaired pit-wheel rumbles into action. *(above)* Andy and Ann Parry.

Historical Context

In 1732, the year that Felin Ganol first appears in official records – around the world, events took place that have meaning to us today and can give us a more complete sense of the time that has passed since a clerk penned that record of a building, already venerable with age.

No. 10 Downing Street is completed in Westminster and becomes the residence of Britain's first Prime Minister, Sir Robert Walpole. His ministry lasted for 21 years.

The Trevi Fountain by sculptor Niccola Salvi is completed in Rome. It has been said that the number and value of coins recovered from the fountain each year is today an "infallible" indictor of the health of the Western economy (and a continuing healthy regard for superstition in our modern scientific age).

Welsh colonist, Morgan Morgan establishes the first permanent settlement in Western Virginia on Mill Creek. Ten years later, coal deposits were found and exploited for the next two centuries.

Benjamin Franklin publishes "Poor Richard's Almanack" which eventually reaches a circulation figure of 10,000. Only the bible will be more widely read in the American colonies. Among its contents were "folksy" urgings to be frugal, industrious and orderly: "God helps those who help themselves", and "never leave 'til tomorrow that which you can do today" are both from Franklin, he credited them to a fictional "Richard Saunders", the "Poor Richard" of the title.

Built almost into the steep bank
The house, traditionally limewashed –
colour on the front, white on the gable
and white on the back.

PANT YR HWCH
(SOW'S HOLLOW), LLANWNNEN, CEREDIGION

The earliest recorded occupier of Pant yr Hwch was Evan David, a "cottager" who died on Christmas Eve in 1699, so by its next recorded mention, as part of the Llysvane estate in 1802, there had been a dwelling on the spot for a century at the very least.

The census of 1841 showed Pant yr Hwch tenanted by Thomas Lewis, who at 55 years old would have been born in 1786, his wife Elizabeth, 15 years his junior and a child called Mary Williams who was ten.

The census records show two properties at Pant yr Hwch and living in the second, were William Williams, farm labourer 30 years old and Sarah Williams his wife 25 years old. Today the remains of the second building, deep in the hollow below Pant yr Hwch itself, show as a footprint of rubblestone giving the shape and extent of William and Sarah's home and are an evocative reminder of how much we lose when there seems no cause to care anymore for these small historic sites.

That footprint will become just a grass covered mound as those natural materials with which it was constructed, become once more part of the earth from where they came. They will then become nothing but a memory, kept alive only by those historically invaluable censuses which every decade from 1841, record the most basic and spare facts, giving us an insight into the lives of those who went before. Those grass covered mounds are little monuments to the human condition. The sites of births, the everyday struggles for survival, the joys, tragedies, triumphs and disasters of life and its eventual inevitable end were all played out within the compass of walls that are all but gone from sight.

In 1851 however William and Sarah were very much alive and had added two daughters to their family, aged ten and five years old, and Pant yr Hwch itself was still the home of Thomas Lewis, who is described as a small-farmer and now 72 years old, his wife Elizabeth and a child lodger aged 11. By 1861 Elizabeth is a widow at 67 and now noted as the farmer and the household, decidedly female, comprised another Elizabeth, who is described as dairy maid, 35 years old and a four month old child named Esther Thomas. Dairy maid Elizabeth's surname was Davies but one could assume that caring for a child so young it was likely that she was the mother.

In the smaller house in the hollow below, William now 49 and Sarah at 42 live with their younger daughter, also Sarah, a scholar aged 14. There is no mention of their elder daughter who by 1861 would have been 20 and would probably have left home. There is always the insipient suggestion working with such sparse information that the disappearance from the census may mean a death, but I prefer to hope that she had moved on to a life of her own.

Another ten years passed and 1871 sees Elizabeth Lewis gone, almost certainly in this case she has died and Elizabeth Davies, the former dairy maid, is now described as the farmer, living with ten year old Esther who is definitively listed as her daughter this time. The reasons for their different surnames and the lack of a husband do not appear of course and it is this kind of anomaly, often occurring in the spare wording of the census, that stirs the imagination, the wondering why and the wish to know more.

Almost certainly Elizabeth Davies had taken over the tenancy on the death of Elizabeth Lewis, her former employer and down below William and Sarah both now in their fifties live on. A grandchild, David Williams, aged five, now with them, but no sign of their daughters who were hopefully living elsewhere with their respective husbands.

1881 and Elizabeth Davies is still farming Pant yr Hwch with her daughter Esther, now 20 and a lodger called Mary Jones, who is described as "unable to work" – another of those bare-boned phrases that can only be fleshed out by the imagination – and William Williams is still the farm labourer at 69 years old,

In proportion
Correct dimensions enhance wood burner placement.

Minimise water ingress
To the rear, alloy gutters are in use to lead rainwater directly into an installed land drain.

Things existing and reinstated

(above) The very unusual design of the stair (see Interiors – Stairs) gains context when seen in its place. Eminently practical 'steps' to overcome a steep and narrow climb. *(above right)* The rebuilt lath and plaster chimney hood that climbs up through the bedroom, to the chimney stack. *(below)* There is no gutter on the front eave of the house – another piece of historical accuracy that works as the overhang of the roof casts the water off perfectly adequately in this case.

living in the second dwelling with Sarah who is 63. Seven years later, before the next census Sarah died at 70 and was buried at Capel y Groes in 1888. She had lived in this tiny house with William since she was 25 and there is little doubt that she died there 45 years later, after a life that we know on a surface level, that can only be scratched by informed speculation, but seems to follow a pattern as ancient as mankind. Young wife, mother of two and grandmother – three stages, each with a thousand implications and each lived out in this little space until the end of her life.

The next census of 1891 mentions the size of Pant yr Hwch for the first time as "of four rooms" with Elizabeth Davies at 63 still farming and living with her daughter Esther Thomas who at 29 now has a one year old son, Daniel Thomas, but seemingly no husband in the house yet again. Mary Jones (unable to work) is still lodging and another child a two year old boarder described as a "nursed child" is added to the household. William Williams is now 78 years old and still named as an agricultural labourer, living in the second dwelling which the census records as consisting of two rooms. Now on his own, a widower, those two rooms must have seemed very empty of life but perhaps full of memories.

William died 11 years after his wife in 1899 when he was 89 years old. Pant yr Hwch must have been a healthy place to live, nearly all who seemed to have died here since 1841 reached a good age for our modern era, let alone a time when there was no affordable medical care or social security blanket for such folk. William reached a remarkable age after a life that can only have consisted of hard physical labour and a simple, probably at times sparse, diet.

1901 and Elizabeth Davies at 74 is still farming Pant yr Hwch with Esther and her grandson Daniel who seems to have reverted to the name of Davies,

abandoning the Thomas surname under which he had been listed since 1871.

Mary Jones still boards with them and the little house in the hollow below is given a name for the first time and a Margaret Evans with her two children, a daughter aged two and son James only eight months old are now living at "Pant yr Hwch Cottage". Yet again no mention of a husband living in the house.

So by 1901 there are no male adults anywhere on the property and everything must have been done by Elizabeth and Esther, with the help of young Margaret Evans. In 1911 Elizabeth Davies is gone and Esther is now described as farmer and Daniel listed as labourer, so Esther has taken on the tenancy. It is ten years since Pant yr Hwch Cottage first acquired a name, though showing unnamed on records for at least a hundred years and also for the first time it appears to be empty.

There is no mention of it after 1911. Its decline to ruin must have begun during that first decade of the twentieth century. Pant yr Hwch itself was still standing and active for in 1931 Daniel Davies is recorded as purchasing 10.631 acres and the house with Hettie Davies, spinster. Hettie is a diminutive of Esther so Daniel at 42 and his mother now 70 become the owners and cease to be mere tenants.

Esther, or Hettie, died in 1943 at 82 and Daniel only four years later at the comparatively young age (especially for Pant yr Hwch) of 58. Here within the records, we have the iceberg tips of two entire lives that began and existed and ended within this house. Esther's recorded life started here in 1861 as the four month old daughter of a servant, the dairy maid and by 1881 has a son herself Daniel, born in 1880. Esther seems to have continued to have worked with her mother, who by 1871 has taken on the tenancy and becomes "farmer" – a climb in status for this little family. So from 1871 onwards this mother, daughter Esther and grandson Daniel farmed Pant yr Hwch as tenants and then in 1931

Inside and out

(above left) Repairs to timberwork, inside and out predominated over replacement. *(above middle)* Historic aperture unaltered, old glass conserved. *(above right)* The new extension – entirely 'in keeping' and 'in character'.

Historical accuracy

(right) The stair leads straight into the bedroom – some would say 'unsuitable for modern life' but others delight in the historical accuracy. The dark patch on the wall is a 'saved' bit of old limewash. *(far right)* New Welsh oak lintel over the repaired simne fawr.

Inside the extension
Lime hemp blocks show behind
the 'workings' of the ground-
source heat pump.

Daniel buys the farm. He is now 42 and his mother 70. Esther lives on with her son at Pant yr Hwch for another 12 years before her life ends in 1943. Quite a lifetime's achievement for Esther then. From daughter of a dairy maid to entitled owner of a farm that leaves her son secure on her death. So Esther's entire life is contained within Pant yr Hwch and Daniel's as well, who farms on until he also dies in 1947. Both were born, lived out their lives and died here. If that does nothing to stir you even a little then perhaps empathy is not your suit.

Between 1947 and 2007 Pant yr Hwch was owned by a family called Kinsella. It appears that during that sixty years the house was only intermittently occupied but by February 2008 it was in the hands of the present owners and those who are responsible for its revival and consequently its now assured material survival into future centuries.

Martin Jones and his wife Ann had a particularly knowledgeable approach to the conservation of Pant yr Hwch. There was no necessity for any explanation by us of the correct function of the various parts of the building.

So the usual removal of modern vapour impermeable materials and their replacement with the "right stuff" restored the natural ability of the building to survive and its conservation was further ensured by the introduction of under floor heating and a ground source heat pump, valuable modern additions to the building's energy performance, already enhanced by sheep's wool insulation and the reinstatement of Pant yr Hwch's ability to benefit from the use of its own thermal mass.

A carefully thought through extension was built onto the gable end, made up of hemp and lime building blocks laid in lime mortar and faced with local rubblestone, also laid and pointed in lime mortar and then limewashed. The use of new genuinely eco-friendly technology and traditional, equally eco-friendly materials create a near perfect scenario – a repaired and conserved historic home

with an extension that is as green as possible and that is completely "in character".

Pant yr Hwch in its shape and its placement of doors and windows differs from the usual and most numerous of patterns for small Welsh vernacular buildings. Its main entrance, or front door, it would appear has always been in a gable end and not in the façade. The door has at some stage in the past become itself enclosed by an extension, which is now the kitchen and the exterior door of this historic extension became the front door of the house. There is no provision for a back door because Pant yr Hwch was built almost into the bank of steeply rising ground behind.

Space has been cleared behind the house and land-drains laid to intercept the natural flow of water drainage and lead it away from the house – a precaution that gives Pant yr Hwch's breathability every chance to function to its maximum.

Inside the configuration of the stair is unusual, not only in the fact that it climbs from the rear to the front (the foot of most stairs faces the façade of the house), but also in its very unusual and delightful design (see illustration).

There was an old ruinous and disused brick built range and oven in place of an obviously removed traditional simne fawr. After some considerable agonising it was decided that it should go and the "great fireplace" be reinstated. A baulk of Welsh oak was re-emplaced where evidence clearly showed its previous existence as the fire hood lintel, and a lathe and plaster chimney hood built above and up through the bedroom to the chimney stack itself.

Repairs to existing timber work predominated and new windows and doors of appropriate design were used where repair was not possible. Interior lime plastering, limecrete floors with traditional breathable surfacing but untraditional under floor heating pipes, limewashed walls throughout and Martin and Ann's knowledgeable attention to detail have made the interior of this building nothing short of a delight. With its historic function and aesthetic returned to the interior we have in Pant yr Hwch a prime example of a highly sustainable, solid-walled, rubblestone structure already standing in its place for at least 300 years, a part of and an enhancement to the landscape – a striking example and asset to the community long into the future.

Attention to detail
(from left to right) Simple blacksmith's hinge. A reproduced 'historical' wooden latch – new, but accurate. An unusual wood burner, designed by Martin and custom made. The bathroom has achieved a comfortable blend of modern and traditional.

Determined conservator
Martin Jones. Martin has begun a careful excavation of Pant yr Hwch Cottage, adding more context to this story.

Historic Context

During the year that Pant yr Hwch's Evan David dies – 1699, the following took place around the world:

The London Stock Exchange (the world's first) completes its first year of trading. Sanctioned by parliament the previous year, Britain's merchants officially enter their first year of slave-trading.

William Dampier explores the West coast of Australia by ship (and finds it "uninspiring") and after rounding the northern coast of New Guinea discovers and names the island of New Britain.

Parliament passes the Woollens Act to prevent any American colony exporting wool, wool yarn or wool cloth to "any place whatsoever", to protect the British wool trade.

At the Drury Lane Theatre – "The Tragical History of King Richard III" is presented by Colley Cibber – an adaptation of the hundred year old (1592) play by William Shakespeare.

Stockholm's Drottingham Palace, a summer residence for the Swedish Royal family, is completed in the style of the French Renaissance.

Dom Pierre Perignon produces sparkling wine (to be called after the region in which he lived – Champagne). He uses a new blend of grapes and "corked bottles of strong English glass".

Pant yr Hwch Cottage
Exposing the quarry tile floor and the edge of the hearth that once warmed William and Sarah and their children and grandchildren – lime plaster and wash still cling to the wall. Part of one wall still stands – now shelter for beehives. The earth and tree covered mound that was a family home.

TWELVE
LIVING THE DREAM

It behoves those of us who champion the cause of historic building conservation to lead by example. We who shout the loudest about the devastating lack of knowledge that causes such unnecessary decay, the entrenched attitudes that encourage ridiculous solutions to the comparatively simple question of the sustainability of old solid-walled buildings and the misleading and often downright false images of historic structures, brought about by an equally ignorant and manipulative media, should be seen to take action.

The aspiration to contribute to the education, training and practical skills that recreate the sustainability inherent in those, almost one half million solid-walled homes in Wales, would be seriously compromised if we lived in modern bungalows. So the correct repair, conservation and inhabitation of our own historic houses are essential if we are to be convincing. Perhaps we go further than others, for our own homes often become examples of the correct actions to

Outside Dolaumaen
Cliff and Katrina Blundell
(left, photo by Barnaby Annan)

Traditional heating
The supplementary woodburning stove, the 'old fashioned' fuel and the pre-war (1936) solid fuel range that provides contstant heat.

take and their consequences, and are visited by potential converts. To teach the dream effectively, we must live it.

Because the lime revival has only been happening for about thirty years and its rise from the ashes was pretty obscure for the first half of those here in Wales, to find properly and comprehensively limed buildings that have been in that condition long enough to form judgements on the material's practical and aesthetic properties as it ages within a domestic situation is rare. The longest continually occupied examples in existence in this part of the world that I'm aware of are my own and my business partner's homes.

There are very often two questions asked, or rather statements made by those who are teetering on the brink of a decision that could make a real difference to their lives. Because lime work (plasters and washes) is of a softer material than modern cementitious plasters and vinyl-based paints, the preconception seems to be that wear will be swiftly evident and "it won't stand up to modern family living". More specifically we hear "we have children – therefore I need a washable surface finish on my walls".

There are some adjustments to be made when living with this historic material, but none are overly onerous and once accepted as simply being a part to play in the sustenance of a dry and healthy home, when the alternative is usually the repetitive appearance of damp and its associated mould, it becomes second nature.

Interior lime plaster is softer than modern plasters, but its resilience is not to be underestimated. When damage occurs it is almost always in predictable places and circumstances.

The base of a wall that has no skirting board can be damaged by enthusiastic use of vacuum cleaners, doors can swing back onto walls and cause damage with their handles, narrow passages can have their walls clipped by the transit of items that are too wide for them. In all those situations, the initial adjustment is obviously awareness and therefore avoidance. One becomes naturally more careful with the base of those walls, door stops will prevent damage caused by swinging doors and if something is not going to fit between the walls of a passage don't try to make it. Bits of damage will obviously occur (as they will in any modern home) but the solution is easy. With limewash one simply waits until there are enough scrapes and bumps to merit mixing up a small tub and reapplying the wash to them all. Damage to plaster is equally easily patched, the only difference being that both the limewash and the plaster usually has to be made up by the repairer. We find it is a simple task to teach those who want to know how to maintain this traditional material in their homes, usually half an hour of instruction will suffice. Now as lime re-emerges into the light of the modern day there are even lime "ready mixes" in re-sealable containers that can be used for repair to everyday wear and tear.

Outside Crug Bach
Chris, Zoe, Louis and Jody Wright

The following two homes that I wish to highlight are examples of comprehensively re-limed properties that have for some years been "lived in" with all the implications that apply to that phrase. One, my own home, is perhaps somewhat more purist in that it has no form of central heating, has historic slate slab floors laid straight onto the earth (no cement concrete beneath or damp proof membrane), the water supply comes from a spring on the mountainside above and warmth for the house and hot water is supplied by that old fashioned method, real flame.

A pre-war (1936 model) solid fuel range provides more than enough constant heat to maintain extremely cosy living conditions in an area of approximately 35sqm and more than enough hot water. A separate room at ground level is heated on demand by a wood burning stove – once laid and lit, the room is warm in ten minutes even on the coldest day. When we have guests from a "centrally heated background" we provide oil filled electric radiators for their bedrooms, only used should they feel the need and bathrooms have heated towel rails and as a back-up but rarely used, wall mounted fan heaters. But the range is the constant, the heart of our home.

Because all of the walls function as they should, as does the floor, this house makes maximum use of the thermal mass of the more than metre thick walls. Removable secondary glazing and the placement of sheep's wool insulation in the roof-space adds to the building's ability to capture and use the heat that is first absorbed and then released by those thermally heavy walls. It works as it

Open fire
The ground floor fireplace generates some extra warmth.

Inside Crug Bach
(far left) Wood burner with the mantleshelf – family identity in a microcosm. *(left)* Solid fuel range that also serves underfloor heating.

should and is consequently a warm, dry and healthy home with a much smaller fuel bill than any solid-walled house of equivalent size that is still struggling against the accelerated decay and the chilling effect of trapped water in its walls.

The second, belongs to my business partner and his wife and is lived in by them and their two small, highly active boys.

This example I offer in answer to that cry of "we have children". This family live in a home, lime plastered and limewashed throughout, and including pre-baby time they have lived there for over a decade.

The house is lime mortar pointed and limewashed outside as you would expect and they also have a solid fuel range, a Rayburn, used for cooking (with a modern back up cooker that sits beside it), hot water and under floor heating. When the heating was proposed, both the company that supplied the under floor pipework, valves and all the other paraphernalia necessary and Rayburn themselves, required a waiver to be signed, releasing them from responsibility should the plan not work. Neither had ever experienced heating of this kind, run by a solid fuel range and were doubtful of its success. This kind of heating is designed to be run by a dedicated boiler and that boiler was expected to be powered by gas or oil, so this was truly pioneering.

It works remarkably well, supplying the kind of background warmth throughout the ground floor that does minimal harm (unlike radiators) to woodwork and the heat from the Rayburn can be used at the same time to warm the kitchen, cook and radiate that particular ambience so relevant to older houses, its solid fuel providing so much more than the single service produced by an isolated central heating boiler. It also means that there are not the eyesores of radiators inside and of a green plastic oil tank or the bunkered industrial shape of a gas tank squatting in the garden, neither of which are truly "in keeping" within the grounds of a rural period property.

If any other rooms need to be warmer, a wood burner in one and a fireplace in the other (on the ground floor) are lit to generate the extra. Again thermal mass, removable secondary glazing and loft insulation, all functioning as they should create conditions of comfort and warmth that suit modern family life perfectly well.

There is of course what may be perceived as a major drawback by some. Solid fuel needs attendance. Logs need chopping, fuel needs to be carried into the house, fireboxes need to be riddled and ashes removed. Fires need to be laid and lit and topped up as you go along. It becomes a routine that itself becomes second nature.

Someone once told me that I make life difficult for myself – all they had to do was flick a switch. They have completely missed the point. The supply of your own fuel, the satisfaction of a full wood shed, the intimate knowledge gained of the foibles of your range or burner and the benefits to your home of the effects of flame, drawing air through the building, and providing the particular kind of heat that enhances its function and does no damage through excessive dry heat shrinkage, are all so relevant to my life that they certainly do not feel like hardships.

The spare almost unconscious act of creating heat by simply flicking a switch seems empty of any real contact with that primary connection man has with fire – another easy, convenient isolation from the truth.

We have been punctilious in not "set-dressing" these two homes, they are as they appear in the illustrations showing the kind of fading and wear one should expect over a decade and more in such houses. Modern family living, children and all, is completely feasible within traditional walls that are finished with traditional materials and in these cases that feasibility is enhanced by the comfort and health levels achieved by reinstating the solid wall's capabilities. Thermal effectiveness at levels that cannot be matched if those walls are abused and malfunctioning. If the house is properly maintained with the "right stuff" then those children may well have children whose children will see this building, still performing efficiently as it should. I have no doubt that to those generations to come, the actions that assured the function of this house will be the norm, and it will be standard practice for all pre-1919 solid-walled structures to be treated thus. I am confident that the power of logic, the blindingly obvious consequences of current muddled thinking will prevail, sooner rather than later, over existing entrenched and commercially prejudiced attitudes that are beneficial only to those that hold them.

DOLAUMAEN (STONY FIELDS)
MYNACHLOGDDU, NORTH PEMBROKESHIRE

The Preselis
Wherein Dolaumaen stands, loom
across the horizon under a huge sky.

The word Dolaumaen has an interesting etymology. In modern Welsh the first element Dol translates as field or enclosure and Maen as stone. In archaic Welsh however Dolau (the plural) meant rings or circles, so in times past Dolaumaen would translate as stone circles or stone rings. Circular enclosures for livestock were the norm in ancient times in these hills and the Dolau element came to mean the angular enclosures that we now called "fields" in English. It is a name older than modern Welsh usage.

Dolaumaen, the house, is on the front cover of this book. Definitive records go back to 1713 with mention of the John family of Dolaumaen in parish records donating services (Overseer of the Poor) and money for poor relief (any annual surplus to be spent on books for the Sunday school), but the house has been in its place for much longer than that and the Johns remained owners of Dolaumaen into the 20th Century.

While carrying out conservation and repair work on the building, it became obvious that it has grown substantially over the centuries from its very humble beginnings as a one room "bwthyn" or cottage. That one room is now the parlour of the existing house.

Dolaumaen has grown at various times in every direction. It has become wider, both the façade and rear of the building moving outwards. It has grown decidedly in length, now incorporating many times the ground area of its first

A rugged historic landscape

(clockwise from top left) Foel Cwm Cerwyn, the mountain of myth and legend. Fertile if boggy ground in the valley floor. The descendants of the natural forestation stand sentinel-like as a windbreak around Dolaumaen.

incarnation and of course upwards from a single storey to two. Those changes seemingly took place before the date that it is shown on record in 1786 as the large and important hill farm that by 1840, sixty years later, was being called the Dolaumaen Estate. This was left on his death by Thomas John, gentleman, in the hands of trustees, with his wife Elizabeth as tenant.

Dolaumaen land centred around the narrow valley of the headwaters of the Eastern Cleddau River. There is some comparatively fertile if boggy ground in the bottom, while steep, rocky highland heath rises from its floor, the jagged ridge of Carn Menin dominating its western margins. Sheep country.

Carn Menin is recognised as the site of the prehistoric quarry where early settlers of these lands extracted the iconic "Bluestones" that form the inner circle of Stonehenge. Bluestone, a spotted dolerite, is one of the resistant igneous masses that remain in ferocious isolation after softer rocks were reduced to clay by the creeping excoriation of the Great Ice Age that followed Preselis' formative earth movement and violent volcanic activity.

Just to the north of this ridge stands the imposingly steep, triple-peaked Foel Drigarn. Not, in spite of initial appearance, a completely natural piece of this rugged landscape, but an iron-age fortress, a place of habitation and defence. To the south, the sweeping bulk of Foel Cwm Cerwyn that peaks at 536 metres, the very top of the Preselis, and a source of myth and tales of the supernatural.

Dolaumaen stands on the lower slopes of Foel Dyrch, which forms the high land of the eastern margin of the valley and from its front windows the whole sweep of the western margins fills the view. It is a magnificent, constantly entrancing aspect, rising beneath a huge sky, the whole enhanced by the palpable sense of human habitation. This landscape is dotted with standing stones, ancient burial chambers, prehistoric trackways and trading routes, places of fortification and ceremony. The remains of a great stone circle, Gorse Fawr, stand a short distance to the south west, where the valley opens onto a broader landscape.

Dolaumaen sits firmly within this glory, as much a part of the tradition of the habitation of this high land as those more ancient reminders. It is built of that same evocative Bluestone, the form of its structure dictated by human necessity,

Local materials from the landscape
(clockwise from top left) The jagged outcrops of Carn Menin – pre-historic bluestone quarry. Local roofing slates, both blue and silver grey. The remains of the Dolaumaen Silver Grey Slate Company's quarry on Foel Dyrch. Local silver and blue slabs used for steps.

its component parts taken from the very land on which it stands, a land long influenced and manipulated by man. A human creation that, because this landscape is no place for towns or for settlements any larger than a few hundred people, and has had no major stimulus for any industry heavier than quarrying or water-driven mills, continues in the truly rural tradition of mankind's use of his surroundings. An unbroken chain to this day.

Dolaumaen was advertised for sale in 1907 as "the Dolaumaen Estate, comprising nine farms, a slate quarry, 650 acres and rights of pasture over a further 2000 acres". In mountain farming country that was a truly substantial holding. The tenant farms, all but two that are now those evocative, mournful, grass and moss covered remains, are separate holdings, most of the land sold off with them and only two of those continue to make a living from farming.

It is a hard land to live off and its singularity of sheep farming means that until natural fibres become once more valued as they should be, and by-products of the diminishing oil industry become more expensive with approaching rarity, sheep farming produces only meat, the once valued fleeces now more expensive to have sheared than they return in market value. Most farmers in these hills need more than one occupation to make a living in modern times, and perhaps even in its heyday, Dolaumaen had an extra string to its bow.

The Dolaumaen Silver Grey Slate Company was formed in 1910. The slate quarry mentioned in the sale details of 1907 is situated over the ridge of Foel Dyrch, on the reverse slope of the mountain to the house. It had been worked intermittently during the 19th Century and evidence shows that small scale production of both roofing slates and slab or flagstones was happening even

Warmth and light

(right) The simne fawr is still used for cooking. *(far right)* A mirror in the right place can enhance both light and space.

Old and slightly bent
But still a useful, attractive sash latch.

earlier. The Arthur Evans, who bought the Dolaumaen Estate in 1907, revived the quarry.

The very name indicates the perceived importance of the colour as an attractive alternative to the already ubiquitous purple/maroon of north Walian Caernarvon slates. These silvery slates, smaller and chunkier than Caernarvon's, along with the greens and blues, can still be found surviving on some roofs. The colour variety in this compact area is, as far as I can discover, unique to Wales in these islands. The quarries worked a volcanic ash slate, akin to English Lake District material, which is famously green and quite unlike the argillaceous mudstone of the northern Welsh quarries.

Competitive pricing proved hard to achieve however and although the product was of good quality mass production in north Wales, and efficient railway transport of those products, proved to be too competitive and the quarry was reported idle by the end of 1912.

The excavation remains, of course, a deep gauge into Foel Dyrch with its consequent waste heaps high upon its eastern slope, another unmissable mark of human manipulation of this landscape.

Dolaumaen is of that landscape and living in this house, surrounded by such steep, rugged wildness – a wildness strongly influenced by ancient peoples – is a privilege not to be lightly valued. There is not much wild land left in these small islands and nearly all of that which we call wild has been brought to its current state by our forebears. These bare, bald mountains once had substantial forestation on their lower slopes and in their valleys. Scots pine, our only native conifer, once provided dark brooding cover and survivors with their progeny still stand sentinel-like as a windbreak around Dolaumaen. Now all but gone,

Twelve years of wear
(right) Do not detract from the warmth and texture of lime plaster and wash.
(far right) Old windows repaired and retained – thoroughly in keeping.

Comfortable inside and magnificent outside
(left) Lighting the family 'photo gallery'. *(middle)* Across the landing. *(right)* Those western margins fill the view.

revealing the land itself as the true reason for its wildness – steep slopes, the black waters of peat bog, great boulders of glacial moraine, soil too thin to grow anything but tussock, reed, heather, bilberry and gorse, all a delight in the modern day to gaze upon in their season but little to provide human sustenance – except the sheep that graze upon them and not many of those per acre.

Man can do no more with this land, so it is thinly populated and we call it wild, though a wildness nearly everywhere touched by long human influence.

In the quietness of a still summer evening or the full fury of a howling, rain-laden south-wester that connection can be sensed in a way that simply does not occur in the noise, turmoil and sensory compression of the human conurbation. We who live in such places are a tiny minority of a population which overwhelmingly will never achieve such an experience and that yearning for the "rural idyll" continues, fed as in the Victorian era that spawned it, by falsehoods and fantasy, by the language of captivity and the notion of escape. "Escape to the country".

To be already a part of that notional freedom is a rare and treasured privilege. When Dolaumaen first appeared on record in 1713, three quarters of the population of Britain supported their lives by the use of the land (G.E. Mingay, the Gentry, Longman 1976, 77-8). By the 1850s that figure had dropped to only one fifth and the Victorian yearning for an ideal rusticity was awakened among many of the remaining four fifths.

In the 2000s that fraction is as tiny as one hundredth and that massive imbalance in popular imagery and opinion is turning "the country" into a perceived playground for the urban masses. Many policy decisions made over rural matters are reached and implemented by minds that are entirely disconnected from the reality of those country matters and are often as restricted

Influenced by man
(top) Foel Drigarn, an iron-age fort.
(bottom) Sheep country.

in the breadth of their views as their own urban horizon. A long time ago, for many years I was a city dweller and a happy one but I am now painfully aware of my own restricted attitudes to "the countryside" at that time. I have experienced both forms of existence and I know where I prefer to live – am I perhaps an unwitting victim of the most modern incarnation of the rural idyll? If that is so, I couldn't be a more willing one.

Historic Context:

In 1713, the year Mr John, gentleman of Dolaumaen, becomes overseer of the poor:

The Treaty of Utrecht ends the War of Spanish Succession, with many of its agreements having direct effects that last to our time:

Louis XIV recognises the Protestant succession in Britain.

Gibraltar, Newfoundland, Acadia (now Nova Scotia) and St Kitts in the Caribbean are all ceded to Britain.

First performances of Te Deum and a Jubilate by George Frederick Handel at St Paul's Cathedral to celebrate the Treaty.

Louis XIV receives a coffee bush as a gift – the bush will be stolen and transported to Martinique, where its descendents will produce a vast industry in the Western Hemisphere, eventually producing 90% of the world's coffee in the Americas.

Scotland's clan Macgregor Chief Rob Roy is outlawed for non payment of a debt. His reaction to this has become legend.

John Arbuthnot's satire of the Duke of Marlborough – "The History of John Bull" goes on sale and introduces the name "John Bull" as a symbol of England. One of Marlborough's descendents, Winston Churchill, will come to personify that symbol in our time.

CRUG BACH (LITTLE TUMP)
PENTREGALAR, NORTH PEMBROKESHIRE

Crug Bach is "over the mountain" from Dolaumaen on the eastern edge of the Preselis, as they drop down to the valley of the infant River Taf.

The first census in 1841 shows Jonah Thomas, aged 20 and Mary his wife aged 19 as the inhabitants, and Jonah is listed as a farmer. The name of the property is almost certainly associated with a bronze age round-barrow, recorded by the Royal Commission on the Ancient and Historical Monuments in Wales, as being 19 metres in diameter and "disturbed". A small mound.

The house was built beside a drovers' road, one of many such historic routes used by stockmen to take their living produce to markets both local and over the border into England, where rapidly developing industry produced ready custom in growing towns and cities. Most of those vital arteries are now faint traces of what they were.

There is a strong verbal tradition that Crug Bach was a "Ty Unnos" and the ages of the young couple first recorded there lend some credence to that suggestion, as does the land on which the house stands. A "Ty Unnos" was an "overnight" house, often the only way that a newly married pair from a poor

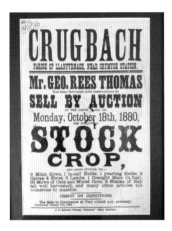

Desperate measures

Farm sale poster. 1879 was a famine year.

As found

(below left) Crug Bach's ruined façade. *(below right)* The rear of Crug Bach as a derelict.

rural background could gain independence and a home of their own.

Uncultivated commonland could be settled upon if certain rules were followed. Those rules were not sanctioned by law, but were enshrined in custom and tradition and were therefore considered a right of the people. Early squatter's rights.

Friends and relations would gather to help meet the customary criteria, the nub of which was that there should be four walls standing, covered by a roof and a fire burning in the hearth by dawn. The new "man of the house" would then stand at the entrance and hurl an axe as far as he could. Where the axe fell marked the boundary of the land which could then be cultivated for sustenance. This is not by any means an entirely Welsh custom, it existed at various times and with various rules throughout the British Isles.

If this verbal tradition concerning Crug Bach is true then the ages of the couple in the census of 1841 would suggest that the house predates the census by only a short span. Of course the Ty Unnos itself would have been most rudimentary and would have been improved upon as soon as resources allowed.

Jonah and Mary obviously made a go of it as records showed that they farmed Crug Bach until they were both well into their sixties and brought up three children, two boys and a girl by dint of their labour. There is a record of a stock sale, what seemed to be Crug Bach's entire assets in 1880, when Jonah was not yet 60. It is perhaps significant that the previous year 1879, saw Britain's and Europe's worst crop failures of the entire century, causing soaring prices that would impact even basic foodstuffs.

We know that Jonah died at 71 in 1892, but Mary's fate remains obscure and Crug Bach itself must have suffered from the law of diminishing returns, and subsistence farming, literally from hand to mouth, probably dominated survival over the next few decades.

The 1911 census makes no mention of Crug Bach or the family, although we

Interior details
(left) The luscious 'red dining room'.
(top) Simple and suitable furnishing.
(bottom) Slate cill – all the above in character and in keeping.

know from the personal recollection of a neighbour that there were Thomases still at Crug Bach in the 1930s and Anna, born to Jonah and Mary in 1856 figures strongly in that recollection. She would have been an old woman in her seventies and eighties during the 1930s and the neighbour, as a young child, thought that she was perhaps a witch. She used to burn the "prickles" off gorse bushes and then collect the woody growth thus exposed for fuel. Her apron, hands and face were always blackened with soot, giving her a somewhat sinister air. He remembers three people living at Crug Bach then; Anna, her husband Llewellyn Davies and one of Anna's brothers, known only as "Tommy Crug Bach".

"We considered ourselves poor," says the neighbour, "but they were really poor." Crug Bach he recalls as a very simple cottage that may have had a "crog lofft" or sleeping platform in the roofspace.

That valuable testimony from the neighbour, who as an adult owned and farmed the holding that bordered Crug Bach from soon after the Second World War to recent years, included another fascinating gem of recollection.

The Thomases of Crug Bach it was said were not in origin, native to Wales. The Thomas who founded the little family group that farmed this difficult piece of land in a difficult time, came overland from the Cornish peninsula. A tin miner who trekked from his birthplace with what goods and chattels he had, including some animals, in a kind of diminutive "wagon train" up to Shrewsbury, his closest bridge crossing of the River Severn. He then headed south west again, seeking work in the then thriving lead and silver mines at

In spite of children
Lime plaster and wash survive well in the comfortable parlour.

Llanfyrnach, only a few miles from Crug Bach which we know was active in the late 18th Century and well into the 19th.

It was not unusual for people with skills that for some reason were becoming redundant in their native place to go wherever that skill was still relevant, sometimes if necessary half way across the world. In this case speculation that racial and linguistic empathy may have had some bearing on the decision of destination adds a touch of extra humanity to this story. The Cornish Peninsula was the West-Walas of the Anglo Saxon Chronicle, even as Wales proper was North-Walas. The particular Celtic of the Welsh language survived then in Cornwall and the Cornish and Welsh (along with the Bretons across the channel) spoke the same tongue and came from the same genetic stock. Mining skills seem also to be a common factor, though this of course was due entirely to the geology of the Western extremities of these islands, which have long been the only substantial suppository of those original inhabitants of Britain, whether Iberian or Celtic, whose lands were wrested from them by English invaders from the continent. Language, blood and mining.

In more recent times, postal records indicate that letters were delivered to Crug Bach in the early 1960s but deliveries then ceased until the ownership of those that now live there.

Crug Bach was bought by Chris Wright's mother in the 1990s, the derelict building and the land, with the intention of repairing the house properly, using traditional materials.

Cynthia Wright was for many years the Estate Manager of Kelmarsh Hall in Northamptonshire, which during her tenure became a local centre for the dissemination of the knowledge and skills required for conserving historic

Built in storage

(right) Cupboard doors 'in keeping' – butt and bead construction enhances suitability. *(far right)* 'We have children!' and dogs live here too – underfloor heating can be very cosy.

buildings, closely associated with the SPAB. On her untimely death in 2000, Crug Bach was inherited by her two sons, still in dereliction.

Chris, his brother Michael and their father William Wright, decided that the house should be repaired as Cynthia would have wished. I was commissioned to oversee those repairs using traditional methods and materials. This was the start of a long and strong association between Chris and me, that resulted in the formation of the Lime Company of West Wales (TLC).

Chris bought his brother's share of the house in 2004, married Zoë and they had two sons, Louis and Jody. Thus they continue the living human story of an historic, Welsh vernacular building. A story that nearly ended with the disappearance of Crug Bach as it returned to the soil like so many before it. But because the desire and will were there to arrest that decay and conserve this little bit of history into a future that could last hundreds of years more, as long as this building is maintained with those traditional materials, this story has not reached "the end".

Historical Context:

In 1841 when Jonah and Mary Thomas were recorded as living at Crug Bach:

The first population census took place in the United Kingdom. A population of 18.5 million is recorded with 15 million of it in England and Wales. London is a city of 2.24 million (Paris – 935,000, Vienna – 357,000, Berlin – 300,000).

Income Tax is introduced in Britain by Robert Peel's Ministry for all who earn over £150 per annum at seven pence in the pound (£1 equals 20 shillings – one shilling equals 12 pence).

Cooks Tours began trading as providers of "temperance holidays".

Thomas Fitzpatrick, trapper and Indian trader, guides the first emigrant wagon train west to Oregon Territory – a two thousand mile journey for 130 settlers through hostile Indian territory. Now a standard image of the "Western".

British soldier Sir James Brooke is confirmed as Rajah of Sarawak by the Sultan of Borneo and will rule as Rajah Brooke until his death in 1868.

Hong Kong is ceded to Britain by China.

New Zealand become a British Colony.

THE LITTLE HOUSE IN THE WOOD
PENCARREG, CARMARTHENSHIRE

Here is something extra, something different to round off this section of the book, by kind permission of Robin Wealans. This very pretty, very traditional and very rare example of a south Walian thatched cottage is a new build. Its existence goes back to 2005, only eight years old at the time of writing, but the methods and materials used to build it are hundreds and hundreds of years old.

Commissioned by a man who has both knowledge of and admiration for those traditions in folk architecture that we conservators strive to maintain, it goes to the heart of the matter by recreating the actions and material use, once so usual in this land.

In our world of building conservation, we should and usually do, know how, and with what, a traditional Welsh cottage of the pre-industrial era was built

and we spend our working lives repairing such buildings using those same methods and materials. But how many of us have built one from the ground up?

This is not a media-influenced fantasy. This is a building that architectural historians could be forgiven for misdating. Craftmanship abounds throughout. The rubblestone work, the use of lime mortars, plaster and limewash and the outstanding beauty of the structural timberwork are all a credit to those who made this house and caused it to be built. The thatch on the roof was once among the most economical of roof coverings and consequently a common sight in this part of Wales on smaller buildings. Perhaps now the most expensive to achieve and thus the most rare of historic roofs, this example of reed thatch with a rye-straw ridge combines both materials used historically in this area.

Over-romanticising historic buildings to impress some sense of their value onto those with little knowledge or concern for them is usually to be avoided, for it can create expectations that are easily disappointed. This is however undeniably a romantic project, almost fairytale like in its appearance, its commission and completion have created something beautiful and eminently practical.

From its breathing limecrete floors, to its stunning structural roof timbers, its lime mortared and washed rubblestone walls, its lime plastered basket work chimney hood and of course its thatch, it emanates a sense of craftsmanship and the sheer joy of achievement is in that sense – this is a house that can be lived in from day to day, not a mere exhibit. This house shows that it can still be done from start to finish, and done properly.

Built deep within private land, away from prying eyes, planning permission was not sought initially. It was thought the usual lack of empathy and

'Historic' details

(left) Thatch continues up and around the chimney, an early and traditional approach to the 'smoke-vent' (see Eurwyn Wiliams, The Welsh Cottage – RCAMW). *(middle)* Limewashed rubblestone walls, laid in lime mortar, surround an appropriate window. *(right)* Looking up the chimney – the modern metal flue provides sensible protection where traditionally an open fire would have burned.

Craftsman, visionary and builder of this house

Steve Medland, member of the Building Limes Forum Training and Education sub-committee, strongly believes that 'you have to be able to do it, to teach it'. He demonstrates and instructs on courses for BLF, SPAB, RICS and CAT.

Tradition rules
(left) From the 'crog lofft' the structural timberwork is a joy to behold. *(middle)* The lime plastered basketwork fireplace hood sits comfortably in surroundings that could be hundreds of years old; slate slab floor, lime plaster and limewash, all combine to stunning effect. *(right)* Delightful detail evident throughout; a shining example of 'how to do it'!

understanding for such a project would colour officialdom's outlook and that thought was very probably correct. However "neighbourly" intervention brought it to the notice of the authorities and having paid a visit and seen this beautiful creation, planning was granted in retrospect and even with some admiration. They could have ordered its demolition.

If planning permission had been sought prior to that witness and building regulations were involved in their heavy handed fashion before its completion, it is doubtful that it would ever have happened – too many boxes un-ticked. In a world full of irony, here is one to be celebrated.

THE FUTURE

The future for the lime revival, I feel, is already written. It is a material that will see increasing use as the current "sustainability-scrummage" settles down to more sensible, clear headed thinking and effective action. Those who have the knowledge and ability to use lime successfully will be in demand, so to learn of its properties and correct use can only be a worthwhile investment.

I suspect however that before an increase in good, effective usage triumphs there is going to be an increase in its misuse by those chasing a quick return who have not bothered to educate themselves adequately, and so in the next few years, we will likely have disappointments to rival the successes.

The more it is used however the more general will become the knowledge of how to use it well and the more economical lime will become to use. Volume of manufacture will increase and market demand will bring down the price as it becomes evident, even to the most reluctant, that the sustainability of our legacy of historic buildings, one third of Wales' housing stock, not to mention all the other pre-1919 buildings in existence that have the potential to add to that housing stock – farm buildings, ecclesiastical buildings, industrial structures and storage facilities – depend on the correct use of lime.

Climate change has already indicated the potential for one of lime's outstanding properties. The wetter summers that we have been experiencing in the last few years have highlighted the vulnerability of huge numbers of buildings to flood risk. A modern cavity wall structure or a cemented up solid-walled building can take months to dry out adequately for rehabitation after a flood. Structures built using lime mortars instead of cement, whether cavity or solid, will dry out through the process of evaporation in a fraction of that time and will require far less intervention and repair before they are once again usable. This has obvious implications for both those living in flood risk areas and the insurance industry.

Lime's relevance to sustainable new-build, the emergence of evidence that the thermal properties of a solid wall of the correct materials can outperform the cavity wall by some margin is already under scrutiny at a level that will result in a move away from cavity construction.

Building materials that we can grow and can be used without high energy processing (hemp, wool, timber, jute) and are renewable, will become the norm, alongside the traditional material that has been at the heart of historic, sustainable, locally produced and recyclable building for over two thousand years in these islands. A material that reabsorbs up to 25% of the CO_2 it produces in its manufacture and at the end of its very long and useful life simply returns to its natural constituents, causing no pollution in its disposal.

There is no directly compatible material and lime will inevitably overcome its detractors, those that have vested interests in high energy manufacture and chemical complex products for the construction industry. Lime will once more take its place as a mainstream material alongside other genuinely eco-friendly products and when it happens, perhaps in my lifetime, I have no doubt that those former detractors will lay claim to the rediscovery of its usefulness.

While we wait, if this book has helped even a very few readers to decide to use lime in one or more of its various forms to reinstate vapour permeability to their pre-1919 solid-walled homes and thus ensure the health and longevity of those buildings, then that will be a few more removed from the huge figure of nearly half a million malfunctioning homes in Wales and added to our comparatively tiny but growing sustainable legacy.

And if a very few of that very few are inspired to achieve the "wholeness" exhibited by the examples in the previous chapter, then a little more beauty will also have been added to this modern world of manufactured mediocrity.

Amen

Nota Bene

Throughout this book, I write of the oil industry's limited horizon. Since completing the text, it now appears that shale-oil is to provide reserves for possibly a hundred years more.
What will that do to the 'sustainability drive' now being rolled out?
Part of the pressure was undoubtedly the perceived limit on oil production and consequent cost increase, and now that pressure is considerably reduced, although the consequences of continued use of oil for energy can only be hugely detrimental to our planet.

FURTHER READING

Repair of Ancient Buildings
A.R. Powys (SPAB) – ISBN 1-89885-601-X

The Welsh House
Iorwerth C. Peate (Llanerch Press) – ISBN 1-86143-132-5

Precious Inheritance
Cliff Blundell – ISBN 1-90596-001-9

Building Limes in Conservation
Ian Brocklebank (Editor) – ISBN 1-87339-495-3

Lime Works
Patrick McAfee (with BLFI) – ISBN 1-90642-908-9

The Green Guide for Historic Buildings
Prince's Regeneration Trust – ISBN 0-11706-844-5

Old House Handbook
Roger Hunt & Marianne Suhr (SPAB) – ISBN 0-71122-772-9

Period Details
Judith H. Miller & Martin Miller (Mitchell Beazley) – ISBN 0-85533-650-1

The Style Source Book
Judith Miller (Mitchell Beazley) – ISBN 1-86732-718-0

The House: Its Origins & Evolution
Stephen Gardiner (Constable) – ISBN 1-84119-244-9

The Conservation Directory (Periodical)
Cathedral Communications Ltd – Tel: 01747 871717

Inform
Technical Conservation Group, Historic Scotland – Tel: 0131 668 8638

USEFUL CONTACTS

The Society for the Protection of Ancient Buildings (SPAB)
37 Spital Square, London E1 6DY
Tel: 020 7377 1644
Web: www.spab.org.uk

Building Limes Forum (BLF)
Glasite Meeting House, 33 Barony Street, Edinburgh EH3 6NX
Web: www.buildinglimesforum.org.uk

The Lime Company of West Wales Ltd (TLC)
Tel: 01239 831147 Web: www.tlcwestwales.co.uk

Tywi Centre
Tel: 01558 824271 Web: www.tywicentre.org.uk

DIY Plastics (UK) (lightweight magnetic fastening secondary glazing)
Till & Whitehead Ltd, Unit 9 Alexandra Court, James St., York YO10 3DP
Tel: 0800 281 639 Web: www.diyplas.co.uk

Inclusion in the above listing which is not comprehensive does not imply any endorsement or approval and no responsibility can be accepted by the author or the publisher for any action taken by any party as a result of any information contained therein. Details of sources of information and guidance, of books and journals, and of heritage and conservation bodies can be found on the websites of the Building Limes Forum (www.buildinglimesforum.org.uk), of the Society for the Protection of Ancient Buildings (www.spab.org.uk), and of English Heritage (www.english-heritage.org.uk), and details of suppliers and craftsmen can also be found on the website of The Building Conservation Directory (www.buildingconservation.com).